EXTRA-ILLUSTRATED EDITION

∴

VOLUME 3
THE CHRONICLES
OF AMERICA SERIES
ALLEN JOHNSON
EDITOR

GERHARD R. LOMER
CHARLES W. JEFFERYS
ASSISTANT EDITORS

SIR FRANCIS DRAKE

Painting, probably by Abraham Janssen, 1594. At Buckland Abbey, Devon, England.

ELIZABETHAN SEA-DOGS

A CHRONICLE OF DRAKE AND
HIS COMPANIONS
BY WILLIAM WOOD

NEW HAVEN: YALE UNIVERSITY PRESS
TORONTO: GLASGOW, BROOK & CO.
LONDON: HUMPHREY MILFORD
OXFORD UNIVERSITY PRESS

1921

PREFATORY NOTE

CITIZEN, colonist, pioneer! These three words carry the history of the United States back to its earliest form in 'the Newe Worlde called America.' But who prepared the way for the pioneers from the Old World and what ensured their safety in the New? The title of the present volume, *Elizabethan Sea-Dogs*, gives the only answer. It was during the reign of Elizabeth, the last of the Tudor sovereigns of England, that Englishmen won the command of the sea under the consummate leadership of Sir Francis Drake, the first of modern admirals. Drake and his companions are known to fame as Sea-Dogs. They won the English right of way into Spain's New World. And Anglo-American history begins with that century of maritime adventure and naval war in which English sailors blazed and secured the long sea-trail for the men of every other kind who found or sought their fortunes in America.

CONTENTS

ILLUSTRATIONS

ELIZABETHAN SEA-DOGS

∵

CHAPTER I

ENGLAND'S FIRST LOOK

In the early spring of 1476 the Italian Giovanni Caboto, who, like Christopher Columbus, was a seafaring citizen of Genoa, transferred his allegiance to Venice.

The Roman Empire had fallen a thousand years before. Rome now held temporal sway only over the States of the Church, which were weak in armed force, even when compared with the small republics, dukedoms, and principalities which lay north and south. But Papal Rome, as the head and heart of a spiritual empire, was still a world-power; and the disunited Italian states were first in the commercial enterprise of the age as well as in the glories of the Renaissance. North of the Papal domain, which cut the penin-

sula in two parts, stood three renowned Italian
cities: Florence, the capital of Tuscany, leading
the world in arts; Genoa, the home of Caboto
and Columbus, teaching the world the science of
navigation; and Venice, mistress of the great
trade route between Europe and Asia, controlling
the world's commerce.

Thus, in becoming a citizen of Venice, Giovanni
Caboto the Genoese was leaving the best home
of scientific navigation for the best home of sea-
borne trade. His very name was no bad creden-
tial. Surnames often come from nicknames;
and for a Genoese to be called *Il Caboto* was as
much as for an Arab of the Desert to be known
to his people as The Horseman. *Cabottággio*
now means no more than coasting trade. But
before there was any real ocean commerce it
referred to the regular sea-borne trade of the
time; and Giovanni Caboto must have either
upheld an exceptional family tradition or struck
out an exceptional line for himself to have been
known as John the Skipper among the many other
expert skippers hailing from the port of Genoa.

There was nothing strange in his being natur-
alized in Venice. Patriotism of the kind that
keeps the citizen under the flag of his own country

was hardly known outside of England, France, and Spain. Though the Italian states used to fight each other, an individual Italian, especially when he was a sailor, always felt at liberty to seek his fortune in any one of them, or wherever he found his chance most tempting. So the Genoese Giovanni became the Venetian Zuan without any patriotic wrench. Nor was even the vastly greater change to plain John Cabot so very startling. Italian experts entered the service of a foreign monarch as easily as did the 'pay-fighting Swiss' or Hessian mercenaries. Columbus entered the Spanish service under Ferdinand and Isabella just as Cabot entered the English service under Henry VII. Giovanni—Zuan—John: it was all in a good day's work.

Cabot settled in Bristol, where the still existing guild of Merchant-Venturers was even then two centuries old. Columbus, writing of his visit to Iceland, says, 'the English, *especially those of Bristol*, go there with their merchandise.' Iceland was then what Newfoundland became, the best of distant fishing grounds. It marked one end of the line of English sea-borne commerce. The Levant marked the other. The Baltic formed an important branch. Thus English trade already stretched out over all the main lines.   Long before Cabot's arrival a merchant prince of Bristol, named Canyng, who employed a hundred artificers and eight hundred seamen, was trading to Iceland, to the Baltic, and, most of all, to the Mediterranean.   The trade with Italian ports stood in high favor among English merchants and was encouraged by the King; for in 1485, the first year of the Tudor dynasty, an English consul took office at Pisa and England made a treaty of reciprocity with Tuscany.

Henry VII, first of the energetic Tudors and grandfather of Queen Elizabeth, was a thrifty and practical man.   Some years before the event about to be recorded in these pages Columbus had sent him a trusted brother with maps, globes, and quotations from Plato to prove the existence of lands to the west.   Henry had troubles of his own in England.   So he turned a deaf ear and lost a New World.   But after Columbus had found America, and the Pope had divided all heathen countries between the crowns of Spain and Portugal, Henry decided to see what he could do.

Anglo-American history begins on the 5th of March, 1496, when the Cabots, father and three sons, received the following patent from the King:

Henrie, by the grace of God, King of England and France, and Lord of Irelande, to all, to whom these presentes shall come, Greeting — Be it knowen, that We have given and granted, and by these presentes do give and grant for Us and Our Heyres, to our well beloved John Gabote, citizen of Venice, to Lewes, Sebastian, and Santius, sonnes of the sayde John, and to the heires of them and every of them, and their deputies, full and free authoritie, leave, and Power, to sayle to all Partes, Countreys, and Seas, of the East, of the West, and of the North, under our banners and ensignes, with five shippes, of what burden or quantitie soever they bee: and as many mariners or men as they will have with them in the saide shippes, upon their owne proper costes and charges, to seeke out, discover, and finde, whatsoever Iles, Countreyes, Regions, or Provinces, of the Heathennes and Infidelles, whatsoever they bee, and in what part of the worlde soever they bee, whiche before this time have been unknowen to all Christians. We have granted to them also, and to every of them, the heires of them, and every of them, and their deputies, and have given them licence to set up Our banners and ensignes in every village, towne, castel,

*yle, or maine lande, of them newly founde. And
that the aforesaide John and his sonnes, or their
heires and assignes, may subdue, occupie, and
possesse, all such townes, cities, castels, and yles, of
them founde, which they can subdue, occupie, and
possesse, as our vassailes and lieutenantes, getting
unto Us the rule, title, and jurisdiction of the same
villages, townes, castels, and firme lande so founde.*

The patent then goes on to provide for a royalty
to His Majesty of one-fifth of the net profits, to
exempt the patentees from custom duty, to ex-
clude competition, and to exhort good subjects of
the Crown to help the Cabots in every possible
way. This first of all English documents connected with America ends with these words:
*Witnesse our Selfe at Westminster, the Fifth day of
March, in the XI yeere of our reigne. HENRY R.*

*To sayle to all Partes of the East, of the West,
and of the North.* The pointed omission of the
word *South* made it clear that Henry had no intention of infringing Spanish rights of discovery.
Spanish claims, however, were based on the Pope's
division of all the heathen world and were by no
means bounded by any rights of discovery already
acquired.

Cabot left Bristol in the spring of 1497, a year after the date of his patent, not with the 'five shippes' the King had authorized, but in the little *Matthew*, with a crew of only eighteen men, nearly all Englishmen accustomed to the North Atlantic. The *Matthew* made Cape Breton, the easternmost point of Nova Scotia, on the 24th of June, the anniversary of St. John the Baptist, now the racial fête-day of the French Canadians. Not a single human inhabitant was to be seen in this wild new land, shaggy with forests primeval, fronted with bold, scarped shores, and beautiful with romantic deep bays leading inland, league upon league, past rugged forelands and rocky battlements keeping guard at the frontiers of the continent. Over these mysterious wilds Cabot raised St. George's Cross for England and the banner of St. Mark in souvenir of Venice. Had he now reached the fabled islands of the West or discovered other islands off the eastern coast of Tartary? He did not know. But he hurried back to Bristol with the news and was welcomed by the King and people. A Venetian in London wrote home to say that 'this fellow-citizen of ours, who went from Bristol in quest of new islands, is Zuan Caboto, whom the English now call a

great admiral. He dresses in silk; they pay
him great honour; and everyone runs after him
like mad.' The Spanish ambassador was full
of suspicion, in spite of the fact that Cabot had
not gone south. Had not His Holiness divided
all Heathendom between the crowns of Spain and
Portugal, to Spain the West and to Portugal the
East; and was not this landfall within what the
modern world would call the Spanish sphere of
influence? The ambassador protested to Henry
VII and reported home to Ferdinand and Isabella.

Henry VII meanwhile sent a little present 'To
Hym that founde the new Isle—£10.' It was
not very much. But it was about as much as
nearly a thousand dollars now; and it meant
full recognition and approval. This was a good
start for a man who couldn't pay the King any
royalty of twenty per cent. because he hadn't
made a penny on the way. Besides, it was followed up by a royal annuity of twice the amount
and by renewed letters-patent for further voyages
and discoveries in the west. So Cabot took good
fortune at the flood and went again.

This time there was the full authorized flotilla
of five sail, of which one turned back and four
sailed on. Somewhere on the way John Cabot

disappeared from history and his second son, Sebastian, reigned in his stead. Sebastian, like John, apparently wrote nothing whatever. But he talked a great deal; and in after years he seems to have remembered a good many things that never happened at all. Nevertheless he was a very able man in several capacities and could teach a courtier or a demagogue, as well as a geographer or exploiter of new claims, the art of climbing over other people's backs, his father's and his brothers' backs included. He had his troubles; for King Henry had pressed upon him recruits from the gaols, which just then were full of rebels. But he had enough seamen to manage the ships and plenty of cargo for trade with the undiscovered natives.

Sebastian perhaps left some of his three hundred men to explore Newfoundland. He knew they couldn't starve because, as he often used to tell his gaping listeners, the waters thereabouts were so thick with codfish that he had hard work to force his vessels through. This first of American fish stories, wildly improbable as it may seem, may yet have been founded on fact. When acres upon acres of the countless little capelin swim inshore to feed, and they themselves are preyed on by leaping acres of voracious cod, whose own rear ranks are being preyed on by hungry seals, sharks, herring-hogs, or dogfish, then indeed the troubled surface of a narrowing bay is literally thick with the silvery flash of capelin, the dark tumultuous backs of cod, and the swirling rushes of the greater beasts of prey behind. Nor were certain other fish stories, told by Sebastian and his successors about the land of cod, without some strange truths to build on. Cod have been caught as long as a man and weighing over a hundred pounds. A whole hare, a big guillemot with his beak and claws, a brace of duck so fresh that they must have been swallowed alive, a rubber wading boot, and a very learned treatise complete in three volumes—these are a few of the curiosities actually found in sundry stomachs of the all-devouring cod.

The new-found cod banks were a mine of wealth for western Europe at a time when everyone ate fish on fast days. They have remained so ever since because the enormous increase of population has kept up a constantly increasing demand for natural supplies of food. Basques and English, Spaniards, French, and Portuguese, were presently fishing for cod all round the waters of

northeastern North America and were even then
beginning to raise questions of national rights that
have only been settled in this twentieth century
after four hundred years.

Following the coast of Greenland past Cape
Farewell, Sebastian Cabot turned north to look for
the nearest course to India and Cathay, the lands
of silks and spices, diamonds, rubies, pearls, and
gold. John Cabot had once been as far as Mecca
or its neighborhood, where he had seen the cara-
vans that came across the Desert of Arabia from
the fabled East. Believing the proof that the
world was round, he, like Columbus and so many
more, thought America was either the eastern
limits of the Old World or an archipelago between
the extremest east and west already known. Thus,
in the early days before it was valued for itself,
America was commonly regarded as a mere ob-
struction to navigation — the more solid the
more exasperating. Now, in 1498, on his second
voyage to America, John Cabot must have been
particularly anxious to get through and show the
King some better return for his money. But he
simply disappears; and all we know is what
various writers gleaned from his son Sebastian
later on.

Sebastian said he coasted Greenland, through vast quantities of midsummer ice, until he reached 67° 30′ north, where there was hardly any night. Then he turned back and probably steered a southerly course for Newfoundland, as he appears to have completely missed what would have seemed to him the tempting way to Asia offered by Hudson Strait and Bay. Passing Newfoundland, he stood on south as far as the Virginia capes, perhaps down as far as Florida. A few natives were caught. But no real trade was done. And when the explorers had reported progress to the King the general opinion was that North America was nothing to boast of, after all.

A generation later the French sent out several expeditions to sail through North America and make discoveries by the way. Jacques Cartier's second, made in 1535, was the greatest and most successful. He went up the St. Lawrence as high as the site of Montreal, the head of ocean navigation, where, a hundred and forty years later, the local wits called La Salle's seigneury 'La Chine' in derision of his unquenchable belief in a transcontinental connection with Cathay.

But that was under the wholly new conditions of the seventeenth century, when both French and English expected to make something out of what are now the United States and Canada. The point of the witling joke against La Salle was a new version of the old adage: Go farther and fare worse. The point of European opinion about America throughout the wonderful sixteenth century was that those who did go farther north than Mexico were certain to fare worse. And — whatever the cause — they generally did. So there was yet a third reason why the fame of Columbus eclipsed the fame of the Cabots even among those English-speaking peoples whose New-World home the Cabots were the first to find. To begin with, Columbus was the first of moderns to discover any spot in all America. Secondly, while the Cabots gave no writings to the world, Columbus did. He wrote for a mighty monarch and his fame was spread abroad by what we should now call a monster publicity campaign. Thirdly, our present point: the southern lands associated with Columbus and with Spain yielded immense and most romantic profits during the most romantic period of the sixteenth century. The northern lands connected with the Cabots did nothing of the kind.

Priority, publicity, and romantic wealth all

favored Columbus and the south then as the memory of them does to-day. The four hundredth anniversary of his discovery of an island in the Bahamas excited the interest of the whole world and was celebrated with great enthusiasm in the United States. The four hundredth anniversary of the Cabots' discovery of North America excited no interest at all outside of Bristol and Cape Breton and a few learned societies. Even contemporary Spain did more for the Cabots than that. The Spanish ambassador in London carefully collected every scrap of information and sent it home to his king, who turned it over as material for Juan de la Cosa's famous map, the first dated map of America known. This map, made in 1500 on a bullock's hide, still occupies a place of honor in the Naval Museum at Madrid; and there it stands as a contemporary geographic record to show that St. George's Cross was the first flag ever raised over eastern North America, at all events north of Cape Hatteras.

The Cabots did great things though they were not great men. John, as we have seen already, sailed out of the ken of man in 1498 during his second voyage. Sly Sebastian lived on and almost saw Elizabeth ascend the throne in 1558.

He had made many voyages and served many masters in the meantime. In 1512 he entered the service of King Ferdinand of Spain as a 'Captain of the Sea' with a handsome salary attached. Six years later the Emperor Charles V made him 'Chief Pilot and Examiner of Pilots.' Another six years and he is sitting as a nautical assessor to find out the longitude of the Moluccas in order that the Pope may know whether they fall within the Portuguese or Spanish hemisphere of exploitation. Presently he goes on a four years' journey to South America, is hindered by a mutiny, explores the River Plate (La Plata), and returns in 1530, about the time of the voyage to Brazil of 'Master William Haukins,' of which we shall hear later on.

In 1544 Sebastian made an excellent and celebrated map of the world which gives a wonderfully good idea of the coasts of North America from Labrador to Florida. This map, long given up for lost, and only discovered three centuries after it had been finished, is now in the National Library in Paris. [1]

---

[1] An excellent facsimile reproduction of it, together with a copy of the marginal text, is in the collections of the American Geographical Society of New York.

Sebastian had passed his threescore years and ten before this famous map appeared. But he was as active as ever twelve years later again. He had left Spain for England in 1548, to the rage of Charles V, who claimed him as a deserter, which he probably was. But the English boy-king, Edward VI, gave him a pension, which was renewed by Queen Mary; and his last ten years were spent in England, where he died in the odor of sanctity as Governor of the Muscovy Company and citizen of London. Whatever his faults, he was a hearty-good-fellow with his boon companions; and the following 'personal mention' about his octogenarian revels at Gravesend is well worth quoting exactly as the admiring diarist wrote it down on the 27th of April, 1556, when the pinnace *Serchthrift* was on the point of sailing to Muscovy and the Directors were giving it a great send-off.

After Master Cabota and divers gentlemen and gentlewomen had viewed our pinnace, and tasted of such cheer as we could make them aboard, they went on shore, giving to our mariners right liberal rewards; and the good old Gentleman, Master Cabota, gave to the poor most liberal alms, wishing them to pray for the good fortune and prosperous success of the *Serchthrift*, our pinnace. And then, at the sign of the Christopher, he and his friends banqueted, and made me and them that were in the company great cheer; and for very joy that he had to see the towardness of our intended discovery he entered into the dance himself, amongst the rest of the young and lusty company— which being ended, he and his friends departed, most gently commending us to the governance of Almighty God.

CHAPTER II

HENRY VIII, KING OF THE ENGLISH SEA

THE leading pioneers in the Age of Discovery were sons of Italy, Spain, and Portugal.[1] Cabot, as we have seen, was an Italian, though he sailed for the English Crown and had an English crew. Columbus, too, was an Italian, though in the service of the Spanish Crown. It was the Portuguese Vasco da Gama who in the very year of John Cabot's second voyage (1498) found the great sea route to India by way of the Cape of Good Hope. Two years later the Cortereals, also Portuguese, began exploring the coasts of America as far northwest as Labrador. Twenty years later again the Portuguese Magellan, sailing for the King of Spain, discovered the strait still known by his name, passed through it into the

[1] Basque fishermen and whalers apparently forestalled Jacques Cartier's discovery of the St. Lawrence in 1535; perhaps they knew the mainland of America before John Cabot in 1497. But they left no written records; and neither founded an oversea dominion nor gave rights of discovery to their own or any other race.

Pacific, and reached the Philippines. There he was killed. But one of his ships went on to make the first circumnavigation of the globe, a feat which redounded to the glory of both Spain and Portugal. Meanwhile, in 1513, the Spaniard Balboa had crossed the Isthmus of Panama and waded into the Pacific, sword in hand, to claim it for his king. Then came the Spanish explorers — Ponce de Leon, De Soto, Coronado, and many more — and later on the conquerors and founders of New Spain — Cortés, Pizarro, and their successors.

During all this time neither France nor England made any lodgment in America, though both sent out a number of expeditions, both fished on the cod banks of Newfoundland, and each had already marked out her own 'sphere of influence.' The Portuguese were in Brazil; the Spaniards, in South and Central America. England, by right of the Bristol voyages, claimed the eastern coasts of the United States and Canada; France, in virtue of Cartier's discovery, the region of the St. Lawrence. But, while New Spain and New Portugal flourished in the sixteenth century, New France and New England were yet to rise.

In the sixteenth century both France and England were occupied with momentous things at home. France was torn with religious wars. Tudor England had much work to do before any effective English colonies could be planted. Oversea dominions are nothing without sufficient sea power, naval and mercantile, to win, to hold, and foster them. But Tudor England was gradually forming those naval and merchant services without which there could have been neither British Empire nor United States.

Henry VIII had faults which have been trumpeted about the world from his own day to ours. But of all English sovereigns he stands foremost as the monarch of the sea. Young, handsome, learned, exceedingly accomplished, gloriously strong in body and in mind, Henry mounted the throne in 1509 with the hearty good will of nearly all his subjects. Before England could become the mother country of an empire overseas, she had to shake off her mediæval weaknesses, become a strongly unified modern state, and arm herself against any probable combination of hostile foreign states. Happily for herself and for her future colonists, Henry was richly endowed with strength and skill for his task. With one hand he welded England into political unity,

crushing disruptive forces by the way. With
the other he gradually built up a fleet the like of
which the world had never seen. He had the
advantage of being more independent of parliamentary supplies than any other sovereign. From
his thrifty father he had inherited what was then
an almost fabulous sum — nine million dollars
in cash. From what his friends call the conversion, and his enemies the spoliation, of Church
property in England he obtained many millions
more. Moreover, the people as a whole always
rallied to his call whenever he wanted other
national resources for the national defence.

Henry's unique distinction is that he effected
the momentous change from an ancient to a
modern fleet. This supreme achievement con-
stitutes his real title to the lasting gratitude of
English-speaking peoples. His first care when
he came to the throne in 1509 was for the safety
of the 'Broade Ditch,' as he called the English
Channel. His last great act was to establish in
1546 'The Office of the Admiralty and Marine
Affairs.' During the thirty-seven years between
his accession and the creation of this Navy
Board the pregnant change was made.

'King Henry loved a man.' He had an uner-

ring eye for choosing the right leaders. He delighted in everything to do with ships and shipping. He mixed freely with naval men and merchant skippers, visited the dockyards, promoted
several improved types of vessels, and always
befriended Fletcher of Rye, the shipwright who
discovered the art of tacking and thereby revolu-
tionized navigation. Nor was the King only
a patron. He invented a new type of vessel
himself and thoroughly mastered scientific gunnery. He was the first of national leaders to
grasp the full significance of what could be done
by broadsides fired from sailing ships against the
mediæval type of vessel that still depended more
on oars than on sails.

Henry's maritime rivals were the two greatest
monarchs of continental Europe, Francis I of
France and Charles V of Spain. Henry, Francis,
and Charles were all young, all ambitious, and all
exceedingly capable men. Henry had the fewest
subjects, Charles by far the most. Francis had
a compact kingdom well situated for a great
European land power. Henry had one equally
well situated for a great European sea power.
Charles ruled vast dominions scattered over both
the New World and the Old. The destinies of

mankind turned mostly on the rivalry between these three protagonists and their successors.

Charles V was heir to several crowns. He ruled Spain, the Netherlands, the Kingdom of the Two Sicilies, and important principalities in northern Italy. He was elected Emperor of Germany. He owned enormous oversea dominions in Africa; and the two Americas soon became New Spain. He governed each part of his European dominions by a different title and under a different constitution. He had no fixed imperial capital, but moved about from place to place, a legitimate sovereign everywhere and, for the most part, a popular one as well. It was his son Philip II who, failing of election as Emperor, lived only in Spain, concentrated the machinery of government in Madrid, and became so unpopular elsewhere. Charles had been brought up in Flanders; he was genial in the Flemish way; and he understood his various states in the Netherlands, which furnished him with one of his main sources of revenue. Another and much larger source of revenue poured in its wealth to him later on, in rapidly increasing volume, from North and South America.

Charles had inherited a long and bitter feud with France about the Burgundian dominions on the French side of the Rhine and about domains in Italy; besides which there were many points of violent rivalry between things French and Spanish. England also had hereditary feuds with France, which had come down from the Hundred Years' War, and which had ended in her almost final expulsion from France less than a century before. Scotland, nursing old feuds against England and always afraid of absorption, naturally sided with France. Portugal, small and open to Spanish invasion by land, was more or less bound to please Spain.

During the many campaigns between Francis and Charles the English Channel swarmed with men-of-war, privateers, and downright pirates. Sometimes England took a hand officially against France. But, even when England was not officially at war, many Englishmen were privateers and not a few were pirates. Never was there a better training school of fighting seamanship than in and around the Narrow Seas. It was a continual struggle for an existence in which only the fittest survived. Quickness was essential. Consequently vessels that could not increase their speed were soon cleared off the sea.

Spain suffered a good deal by this continuous

raiding. So did the Netherlands. But such was the power of Charles that, although his navies were much weaker than his armies, he yet was able to fight by sea on two enormous fronts, first, in the Mediterranean against the Turks and other Moslems, secondly, in the Channel and along the coast, all the way from Antwerp to Cadiz. Nor did the left arm of his power stop there; for his fleets, his transports, and his merchantmen ranged the coasts of both Americas from one side of the present United States right round to the other.

Such, in brief, was the position of maritime Europe when Henry found himself menaced by the three Roman Catholic powers of Scotland, France, and Spain. In 1533 he had divorced his first wife, Catherine of Aragon, thereby defying the Pope and giving offence to Spain. He had again defied the Pope by suppressing the monasteries and severing the Church of England from the Roman discipline. The Pope had struck back with a bull of excommunication designed to make Henry the common enemy of Catholic Europe.

Henry had been steadily building ships for years. Now he redoubled his activity. He blooded the fathers of his daughter's sea-dogs by smashing up a pirate fleet and sinking a flotilla of Flemish privateers. The mouth of the Scheldt, in 1539, was full of vessels ready to take a hostile army into England. But such a fighting fleet prepared to meet them that Henry's enemies forbore to strike.

In 1539, too, came the discovery of the art of tacking, by Fletcher of Rye, Henry's shipwright friend, a discovery forever memorable in the annals of seamanship. Never before had any kind of craft been sailed a single foot against the wind. The primitive dugout on which the prehistoric savage hoisted the first semblance of a sail, the ships of Tarshish, the Roman transport in which St. Paul was wrecked, and the Spanish caravels with which Columbus sailed to worlds unknown, were, in principle of navigation, all the same. But now Fletcher ran out his epoch-making vessel, with sails trimmed fore and aft, and dumbfounded all the shipping in the Channel by beating his way to windward against a good stiff breeze. This achievement marked the dawn of the modern sailing age.

And so it happened that in 1545 Henry, with a new-born modern fleet, was able to turn defiantly on Francis. The English people rallied

magnificently to his call. What was at that time
an enormous army covered the lines of advance
on London. But the fleet, though employing
fewer men, was relatively a much more important
force than the army; and with the fleet went
Henry's own headquarters. His lifelong interest
in his navy now bore the first-fruits of really
scientific sea power on an oceanic scale. There
was no great naval battle to fix general attention
on one dramatic moment. Henry's strategy and
tactics, however, were new and full of promise.
He repeated his strategy of the previous war by
sending out a strong squadron to attack the base
at which the enemy's ships were then assembling;
and he definitely committed the English navy,
alone among all the navies in the world, to sailing-
ship tactics, instead of continuing those founded
on the rowing galley of immemorial fame. The
change from a sort of floating army to a really
naval fleet, from galleys moved by oars and depending on boarders who were soldiers, to ships
moved by sails and depending on their broadside
guns — this change was quite as important as
the change in the nineteenth century from sails
and smooth-bores to steam and rifled ordnance.
It was, indeed, from at least one commanding

point of view, much more important; for it meant that England was easily first in developing the only kind of navy which would count in any struggle for oversea dominion after the discovery of America had made sea power no longer a question of coasts and landlocked waters but of all the outer oceans of the world.

The year that saw the birth of modern sea power is a date to be remembered in this history; for 1545 was also the year in which the mines of Potosi first aroused the Old World to the riches of the New; it was the year, too, in which Sir Francis Drake was born. Moreover, there was another significant birth in this same year. The parole aboard the Portsmouth fleet was *God save the King!* The answering countersign was *Long to reign over us!* These words formed the nucleus of the national anthem now sung round all the Seven Seas. The anthems of other countries were born on land. *God save the King!* sprang from the navy and the sea.

The Reformation quickened seafaring life in many ways. After Henry's excommunication every Roman Catholic crew had full Papal sanction for attacking every English crew that would

not submit to Rome, no matter how Catholic its
faith might be. Thus, in addition to danger from
pirates, privateers, and men-of-war, an English
merchantman had to risk attack by any one who
was either passionately Roman or determined to
use religion as a cloak. Raids and reprisals grew
apace. The English were by no means always
lambs in piteous contrast to the Papal wolves.
Rather, it might be said, they took a motto from
this true Russian proverb: 'Make yourself a
sheep and you'll find no lack of wolves.' But,
rightly or wrongly, the general English view was
that the Papal attitude was one of attack while
their own was one of defence. Papal Europe of
course thought quite the reverse.

Henry died in 1547, and the Lord Protector
Somerset at once tried to make England as Protestant as possible during the minority of Edward
VI, who was not yet ten years old. This brought
every English seaman under suspicion in every
Spanish port, where the Holy Office of the Inquisition was a great deal more vigilant and business-
like than the Custom House or Harbor Master.
Inquisitors had seized Englishmen in Henry's
time. But Charles had stayed their hand. Now
that the ruler of England was an open heretic, who

appeared to reject the accepted forms of Catholic belief as well as the Papal forms of Roman discipline, the hour had come to strike. War would have followed in ordinary times. But the Reformation had produced a cross-division among the subjects of all the Great Powers. If Charles went to war with a Protestant Lord Protector of England then some of his own subjects in the Netherlands would probably revolt. France had her Huguenots; England her ultra-Papists; Scotland some of both kinds. Every country had an unknown number of enemies at home and friends abroad. All feared war.

Somerset neglected the navy. But the seafaring men among the Protestants, as among those Catholics who were anti-Roman, took to privateering more than ever. Nor was exploration forgotten. A group of merchant-adventurers sent Sir Hugh Willoughby to find the Northeast Passage to Cathay. Willoughby's three ships were towed down the Thames by oarsmen dressed in sky-blue jackets. As they passed the palace at Greenwich they dipped their colors in salute. But the poor young king was too weak to come to the window. Willoughby met his death in Lapland. But Chancellor, his second-in-command, got through to the White Sea, pushed on overland to Moscow, and returned safe in 1554, when Queen Mary was on the throne. Next year, strange to say, the charter of the new Muscovy Company was granted by Philip of Armada fame, now joint sovereign of England with his newly married wife, soon to be known as 'Bloody Mary.' One of the directors of the company was Lord Howard of Effingham, father of Drake's Lord Admiral, while the governor was our old friend Sebastian Cabot, now in his eightieth year. Philip was Crown Prince of the Spanish Empire, and his father, Charles V, was very anxious that he should please the stubborn English; for if he could only become both King of England and Emperor of Germany he would rule the world by sea as well as land. Philip did his ineffective best: drank English beer in public as if he liked it and made his stately Spanish courtiers drink it too and smile. He spent Spanish gold, brought over from America, and he got the convenient kind of Englishmen to take it as spy-money for many years to come. But with it he likewise sowed some dragon's teeth. The English sea-dogs never forgot the iron chests of Spanish New-World gold, and presently began to wonder whether there was no sure way in far America by which to get it for themselves.

In the same year, 1555, the Marian attack on English heretics began and the sea became safer than the land for those who held strong anti-Papal views. The Royal Navy was neglected even more than it had been lately by the Lord Protector. But fighting traders, privateers, and pirates multiplied. The seaports were hotbeds of hatred against Mary, Philip, Papal Rome, and Spanish Inquisition. In 1556 Sebastian Cabot reappears, genial and prosperous as ever, and dances out of history at the sailing of the *Serchthrift*, bound northeast for Muscovy. In 1557 Philip came back to England for the last time and manœuvred her into a war which cost her Calais, the last English foothold on the soil of France. During this war an English squadron joined Philip's vessels in a victory over the French off Gravelines, where Drake was to fight the Armada thirty years later.

This first of the two battles fought at Gravelines brings us down to 1558, the year in which Mary died, Elizabeth succeeded her, and a very different English age began.

CHAPTER III

LIFE AFLOAT IN TUDOR TIMES

Two stories from Hakluyt's *Voyages* will illustrate what sort of work the English were attempting in America about 1530, near the middle of King Henry's reign. The success of 'Master Haukins' and the failure of 'Master Hore' are quite typical of several other adventures in the New World.

'Olde M. William Haukins of Plimmouth, a man for his wisdome, valure, experience, and skill in sea causes much esteemed and beloved of King Henry the eight, and being one of the principall Sea Captaines in the West partes of England in his time, not contented with the short voyages commonly then made onely to the knowen coastes of Europe, armed out a tall and goodlie ship of his owne, of the burthen of 250 tunnes, called the Pole of Plimmouth, wherewith he made three long and famous voyages vnto the coast of Brasill, a thing in those days very rare, especially to our

Nation.' Hawkins first went down the Guinea Coast of Africa, 'where he trafiqued with the Negroes, and tooke of them Oliphants' teeth, and other commodities which that place yeeldeth; and so arriving on the coast of Brasil, used there such discretion, and behaved himselfe so wisely with those savage people, that he grew into great familiaritie and friendship with them. Insomuch that in his 2 voyage one of the savage kings of the Countrey of Brasil was contented to take ship with him, and to be transported hither into England. This kinge was presented unto King Henry 8. The King and all the Nobilitie did not a little marvel; for in his cheeks were holes, and therein small bones planted, which in his Countrey was reputed for a great braverie.' The poor Brazilian monarch died on his voyage back, which made Hawkins fear for the life of Martin Cockeram, whom he had left in Brazil as a hostage. However, the Brazilians took Hawkins's word for it and released Cockeram, who lived another forty years in Plymouth. 'Olde M. William Haukins' was the father of Sir John Hawkins, Drake's companion in arms, whom we shall meet later. He was also the grandfather of Sir Richard Hawkins, another naval

hero, and of the second William Hawkins, one
of the founders of the greatest of all chartered companies, the Honourable East India
Company.

Hawkins knew what he was about. 'Master
Hore' did not. Hore was a well-meaning, plaus-
ible fellow, good at taking up new-fangled ideas,
bad at carrying them out, and the very cut of a
wildcat company-promoter, except for his honesty.
He persuaded 'divers young lawyers of the Innes
of Court and Chancerie' to go to Newfoundland.
A hundred and twenty men set off in this modern
ship of fools, which ran into Newfoundland at
night and was wrecked. There were no provisions;
and none of the 'divers lawyers' seems to have
known how to catch a fish. After trying to live
on wild fruit they took to eating each other, in
spite of Master Hore, who stood up boldly and
warned them of the 'Fire to Come.' Just then
a French fishing smack came in; whereupon
the lawyers seized her, put her wretched crew
ashore, and sailed away with all the food
she had. The outraged Frenchmen found another vessel, chased the lawyers back to England, and laid their case before the King, who,
'out of his Royall Bountie,' reimbursed the

Frenchmen and let the 'divers lawyers' go scot free.

Hawkins and Hore, and others like them, were the heroes of travellers' tales. But what was the ordinary life of the sailor who went down to the sea in the ships of the Tudor age? There are very few quite authentic descriptions of life afloat before the end of the sixteenth century; and even then we rarely see the ship and crew about their ordinary work. Everybody was all agog for marvellous discoveries. Nobody, least of all a seaman, bothered his head about describing the daily routine on board. We know, however, that it was a lot of almost incredible hardship. Only the fittest could survive. Elizabethan landsmen may have been quite as prone to mistake comfort for civilization as most of the world is said to be now. Elizabethan sailors, when afloat, most certainly were not; and for the simple reason that there was no such thing as real comfort in a ship.

Here are a few verses from the oldest genuine English sea-song known. They were written down in the fifteenth century, before the discovery of America, and were probably touched up a little

by the scribe. The original manuscript is now in
Trinity College, Cambridge. It is a true nautical
composition — a very rare thing indeed; for genuine sea-songs didn't often get into print and
weren't enjoyed by landsmen when they did.
The setting is that of a merchantman carrying
passengers whose discomforts rather amuse the
'schippemenne.'

> Anon the master commandeth fast
> To his ship-men in all the hast[e],
> To dresse them [line up] soon about the mast
>   Their takeling to make.

> With *Howe! Hissa!* then they cry,
> 'What howe! mate thou standest too nigh,
> Thy fellow may not haul thee by:'
>   Thus they begin to crake [shout].

> A boy or twain anon up-steyn [go aloft]
> And overthwart the sayle-yerde leyn [lie]
> *Y-how! taylia!* the remnant cryen [cry]
>   And pull with all their might.

> Bestow the boat, boat-swain, anon,
> That our pylgrymms may play thereon;
> For some are like to cough and groan
>   Ere it be full midnight.

Haul the bowline!   Now veer the sheet!
Cook, make ready anon our meat!
Our pylgrymms have no lust to eat:
      I pray God give them rest.

Go to the helm!   What ho! no neare[r]!
Steward, fellow! a pot of beer!
Ye shall have, Sir, with good cheer,
      Anon all of the best.

Y-howe!   *Trussa!*   Haul in the brailes!
Thou haulest not!   By God, thou failes[t].
O see how well our good ship sails!
      And thus they say among.

   .   .   .   .   .   .

Thys meane'whyle the pylgrymms lie,
And have their bowls all fast them by,
And cry after hot malvesy —
      'Their health for to restore.'

   .   .   .   .   .   .

Some lay their bookys on their knee,
And read so long they cannot see.
'Alas! mine head will split in three!'
      Thus sayeth one poor wight.

   .   .   .   .   .   .

A sack of straw were there right good;
For some must lay them in their hood:
I had as lief be in the wood,
      Without or meat or drink!

> For when that we shall go to bed,
> The pump is nigh our beddës head:
> A man he were as good be dead
>   As smell thereof the stynke!

Howe—hissa! is still used aboard deepwater-men as *Ho — hissa!* instead of *Ho — hoist away! What ho, mate!* is also known afloat, though dying out. *Y-howe! taylia!* is *Yo — ho! tally!* or *Tally and belay!* which means hauling aft and making fast the sheet of a mainsail or foresail. *What ho! no nearer!* is *What ho! no higher* now. But old salts remember *no nearer!* and it may be still extant. Seasickness seems to have been the same as ever — so was the desperate effort to pretend one was not really feeling it:

> And cry after hot malvesy—
>   'Their health for to restore.'

Here is another sea-song, one sung by the sea-dogs themselves. The doubt is whether the *Martial-men* are Navy men, as distinguished from merchant-service men aboard a king's ship, or whether they are soldiers who want to take all sailors down a peg or two. This seems the more

probable explanation. Soldiers 'ranked' sailors
afloat in the sixteenth century; and Drake's was
the first fleet in the world in which seamen-
admirals were allowed to fight a purely naval
action.

We be three poor Mariners, newly come from the Seas,
We spend our lives in jeopardy while others live at ease.
We care not for those Martial-men that do our states
    disdain,
But we care for those Merchant-men that do our states
    maintain.

A third old sea-song gives voice to the universal
complaint that landsmen cheat sailors who come
home flush of gold.

For Sailors they be honest men,
    And they do take great pains,
But Land-men and ruffling lads
    Do rob them of their gains.

Here, too, is some *Cordial Advice* against the
wiles of the sea, addressed *To all rash young Men,
who think to Advance their decaying Fortunes by
Navigation*, as most of the sea-dogs (and gentlemen-
adventurers like Gilbert, Raleigh, and Cavendish)
tried to do.

> You merchant men of Billingsgate,
>   I wonder how you thrive.
> You bargain with men for six months
>   And pay them but for five.

This was an abuse that took a long time to die
out. Even well on in the nineteenth century,
and sometimes even on board of steamers, victualling was only by the lunar month though
service went by the calendar.

> A cursed cat with thrice three tails
>   Doth much increase our woe

is a poetical way of putting another seaman's
grievance.

People who regret that there is such a dis-
crepancy between genuine sea-songs and shore-
going imitations will be glad to know that the
Mermaid is genuine, though the usual air to which
it was sung afloat was harsh and decidedly inferior
to the one used ashore. This example of the
old 'fore-bitters' (so-called because sung from the
fore-bitts, a convenient mass of stout timbers
near the foremast) did not luxuriate in the repeti-
tions of its shore-going rival: *With a comb and a
glass in her hand, her hand, her hand*, etc.

Solo.   On Friday morn as we set sail
      It was not far from land,
      Oh, there I spied a fair pretty maid
      With a comb and a glass in her hand.

Chorus.   The stormy winds did blow,
      And the raging seas did roar,
      While we poor Sailors went to the tops
      And the land lubbers laid below.

The anonymous author of a curious composition entitled *The Complaynt of Scotland*, written in 1548, seems to be the only man who took more interest in the means than in the ends of seamanship. He was undoubtedly a landsman. But he loved the things of the sea; and his work is well worth reading as a vocabulary of the lingo that was used on board a Tudor ship. When the seamen sang it sounded like 'an echo in a cave.' Many of the outlandish words were Mediterranean terms which the scientific Italian navigators had brought north. Others were of Oriental origin, which was very natural in view of the long connection between East and West at sea. Admiral, for instance, comes from the Arabic for a commander-in-chief. *Amir-al-bahr* means commander of the sea. Most of the nautical technicalities would strike a seaman of the present day as being quite modern. The sixteenth-century skipper would be readily understood by a twentieth-century helmsman in the case of such orders as these: *Keep full and by! Luff! Con her! Steady! Keep close!* Our modern sailor in the navy, however, would be hopelessly lost in trying to follow directions like the following: *Make ready your cannons, middle culverins, bastard culverins, falcons, sakers, slings, headsticks, murderers, passevolants, bazzils, dogges, crook arquebusses, calivers, and hail shot!*

Another look at life afloat in the sixteenth century brings us once more into touch with America; for the old sea-dog DIRECTIONS FOR THE TAKYNG OF A PRIZE were admirably summed up in *The Seaman's Grammar*, which was compiled by 'Captaine John Smith, sometime Governour of Virginia and Admiral of New England' — 'Pocahontas Smith,' in fact.

'A sail!'

'How bears she? To-windward or lee-ward? Set him by the compass!'

'Hee stands right a-head' (*or* On the weather-bow, *or* lee-bow).

'Let fly your colours!' (if you have a consort —else not). 'Out with all your sails! A steadie man at the helm! Give him chace!'

'Hee holds his owne — No, wee gather on him, Captaine!'

Out goes his flag and pendants, also his waist-cloths and top-armings, which is a long red cloth . . . that goeth round about the shippe on the out-sides of all her upper works and fore and main-tops, as well for the countenance and grace of the shippe as to cover the men from being seen. He furls and slings his main-yard. In goes his sprit-sail. Thus they strip themselves into their fighting sails, which is, only the foresail, the main and fore topsails, because the rest should not be fired nor spoiled; besides, they would be troublesome to handle, hinder our sights and the using of our arms.

'He makes ready his close-fights, fore and aft.' [Bulkheads set up to cover men under fire] . . .

'Every man to his charge! Dowse your top-sail to salute him for the sea! Hail him with a noise of trumpets!'

'Whence is your ship?'

'Of Spain — whence is yours?'

'Of England.'

'Are you merchants or men of war?'

'We are of the Sea!'

He waves us to leeward with his drawn sword,

*calls out 'Amain' for the King of Spain, and springs
his luff* [brings his vessel close by the wind].

'Give him a chase-piece with your broadside,
and run a good berth a-head of him!'

'Done, done!'

'We have the wind of him, and now he tacks
about!'

'Tack about also and keep your luff! Be yare
at the helm! Edge in with him! Give him a
volley of small shot, also your prow and broadside
as before, and keep your luff!'

'He pays us shot for shot!'

'Well, we shall requite him!' . . .

'Edge in with him again! Begin with your
bow pieces, proceed with your broad-side, and
let her fall off with the wind to give him also
your full chase, your weather-broad-side, and
bring her round so that the stern may also dis-
charge, and your tacks close aboard again!' . . .

'The wind veers, the sea goes too high to board
her, and we are shot through and through, and
between wind and water.'

'Try the pump! Bear up the helm! Sling a
man overboard to stop the leaks, *that is*, truss
him up around the middle in a piece of canvas
and a rope, with his arms at liberty, with a mallet

and plugs lapped in oakum and well tarred, and a tar-pauling clout, which he will quickly beat into the holes the bullets made.'

'What cheer, Mates, is all Well?'

'All's well!'

'Then make ready to bear up with him again!'

'With all your great and small shot charge him, board him thwart the hawse, on the bow, midships, or, rather than fail, on his quarter; or make fast your grapplings to his close-fights and sheer off' [which would tear his cover down].

'Captain, we are foul of each other and the ship is on fire!'

'Cut anything to get clear and smother the fire with wet cloths!'

In such a case they will bee presentlie such friends as to help one the other all they can to get clear, lest they should both burn together and so sink: and, if they be generous, and the fire be quenched, they will drink kindly one to the other, heave their canns over-board, and begin again as before. . . .

'Chirurgeon, look to the wounded, and wind up the slain, and give them three guns for their funerals! Swabber, make clean the ship! Purser, record their names! Watch, be vigilant to keep your berth to windward, that we lose him not in

the night! Gunners, spunge your ordnance!
Souldiers, scour your pieces! Carpenters, about
your leaks! Boatswain and the rest, repair sails
and shrouds! Cook, see you observe your directions against the morning watch!' . . .

'Boy, hallo! is the kettle boiled?'

'Ay, ay, Sir!'

'Boatswain, call up the men to prayer and
breakfast!' . . .

*Always have as much care to their wounded as
to your own; and if there be either young women
or aged men, use them nobly* . . .

'Sound drums and trumpets: SAINT GEORGE FOR
MERRIE ENGLAND!'

CHAPTER IV

ELIZABETHAN ENGLAND

ELIZABETHAN England is the motherland, the true historic home, of all the different peoples who speak the sea-borne English tongue. In the reign of Elizabeth there was only one English-speaking nation. This nation consisted of a bare five million people, fewer than there are to-day in London or New York. But hardly had the Great Queen died before Englishmen began that colonizing movement which has carried their language the whole world round and established their civilization in every quarter of the globe. Within three centuries after Elizabeth's day the use of English as a native speech had grown quite thirtyfold. Within the same three centuries the number of those living under laws and institutions derived from England had grown a hundredfold.

The England of Elizabeth was an England of

great deeds, but of greater dreams. Elizabethan literature, take it for all in all, has never been surpassed; myriad-minded Shakespeare remains unequalled still. Elizabethan England was indeed 'a nest of singing birds.' Prose was often far too pedestrian for the exultant life of such a mighty generation. As new worlds came into their expectant ken, the glowing Elizabethans wished to fly there on the soaring wings of verse. To them the tide of fortune was no ordinary stream but the 'white-maned, proud, neck-arching tide' that bore adventurers to sea 'with pomp of waters unwithstood.'

The goodly heritage that England gave her offspring overseas included Shakespeare and the English Bible. The Authorized Version entered into the very substance of early American life. There was a marked difference between Episcopalian Virginia and Puritan New England. But both took their stand on this version of the English Bible, in which the springs of Holy Writ rejoiced to run through channels of Elizabethan prose. It is true that Elizabeth slept with her fathers before this book of books was printed, and that the first of the Stuarts reigned in her stead. Nevertheless the Authorized Version is pure Elizabethan.

4

All its translators were Elizabethans, as their dedication to King James, still printed with every copy, gratefully acknowledges in its reference to 'the setting of that bright Occidental Star, Queen Elizabeth of most happy memory.'

These words of the reverend scholars contain no empty compliment. Elizabeth was a great sovereign and, in some essential particulars, a very great national leader. This daughter of Henry VIII and his second wife, Anne Boleyn the debonair, was born a heretic in 1533. Her father was then defying both Spain and the Pope. Within three years after her birth her mother was beheaded; and by Act of Parliament Elizabeth herself was declared illegitimate. She was fourteen when her father died, leaving the kingdom to his three children in succession, Elizabeth being the third. Then followed the Protestant reign of the boy-king Edward VI, during which Elizabeth enjoyed security; then the Catholic reign of her Spanish half-sister, 'Bloody Mary,' during which her life hung by the merest thread.

At first, however, Mary concealed her hostility to Elizabeth because she thought the two daughters of Henry VIII ought to appear together in her

triumphal entry into London. From one point
of view — and a feminine one at that — this was
a fatal mistake on Mary's part: for never did
Elizabeth show to more advantage. She was
just under twenty, while Mary was nearly twice
her age. Mary had, indeed, provided herself
with one good foil in the person of Anne of Cleves,
the 'Flemish mare' whose flat coarse face and
lumbering body had disgusted King Henry thirteen years before, when Cromwell had foisted
her upon him as his fourth wife. But with poor,
fat, straw-colored Anne on one side, and black-
and-sallow, foreign-looking, man-voiced Mary
on the other, the thoroughly English Princess
Elizabeth took London by storm on the spot.
Tall and majestic, she was a magnificent example
of the finest Anglo-Norman type. Always 'the
glass of fashion' and then the very 'mould of
form' her splendid figure looked equally well on
horseback or on foot. A little full in the eye,
and with a slightly aquiline nose, she appeared,
as she really was, keenly observant and commanding. Though these two features just prevented her from being a beauty, the bright blue
eyes and the finely chiselled nose were themselves
quite beautiful enough. Nor was she less taking

to the ear than to the eye; for, in marked contrast to gruff foreign Mary and wheezy foreign Anne, she had a rich, clear, though rather too loud, English voice. When the Court reined up and dismounted, Elizabeth became even more the centre of attraction. Mary marched stiffly on. Anne plodded after. But as for Elizabeth — perfect in dancing, riding, archery, and all the sports of chivalry — 'she trod the ling like a buck in spring, and she looked like a lance in rest.'

When Elizabeth succeeded Mary in the autumn of 1558, she had dire need of all she had learnt in her twenty-five years of adventurous life. Fortunately for herself and, on the whole, most fortunately for both England and America, she had a remarkable power of inspiring devotion to the service of their queen and country in men of both the cool and ardent types; and this long after her personal charms had gone. Government, religion, finance, defence, and foreign affairs were in a perilous state of flux, besides which they have never been more distractingly mixed up with one another. Henry VII had saved money for twenty-five years. His three successors had spent it lavishly for fifty. Henry VIII had kept the Church Catholic in ritual while making it purely national in government. The Lord Protector Somerset had made it as Protestant as possible under Edward VI. Mary had done her best to bring it back to the Pope. Home affairs were full of doubts and dangers, though the great mass of the people were ready to give their handsome young queen a fair chance and not a little favor. Foreign affairs were worse. France was still the hereditary enemy; and the loss of Calais under Mary had exasperated the whole English nation. Scotland was a constant menace in the north. Spain was gradually changing from friend to foe. The Pope was disinclined to recognize Elizabeth at all.

To understand how difficult her position was we must remember what sort of constitution England had when the germ of the United States was forming. The Roman Empire was one constituent whole from the emperor down. The English-speaking peoples of to-day form constituent wholes from the electorate up. In both cases all parts were and are in constant relation to the whole. The case of Elizabethan England, however, was very different. There was neither despotic unity from above nor democratic unity from below, but a mixed and fluctuating kind of government in which Crown, nobles, parliament, and people formed certain parts which had to be put together for each occasion. The accepted general idea was that the sovereign, supreme as an individual, looked after the welfare of the country in peace and war so far as the Crown estates permitted; but that whenever the Crown resources would not suffice then the sovereign could call on nobles and people for whatever the common weal required. *Noblesse oblige.* In return for the estates or monopolies which they had acquired the nobles and favored commoners were expected to come forward with all their resources at every national crisis precisely as the Crown was expected to work for the common weal at all times. When the resources of the Crown and favored courtiers sufficed, no parliament was called; but whenever they had to be supplemented then parliament met and voted whatever it approved. Finally, every English freeman was required to do his own share towards defending the country in time of need, and he was further required to know the proper use of arms.

The great object of every European court during early modern times was to get both the old feudal nobility and the newly promoted commoners to revolve round the throne as round the centre of their solar system. By sheer force of character — for the Tudors had no overwhelming army like the Roman emperors' — Henry VIII had succeeded wonderfully well. Elizabeth now had to piece together what had been broken under Edward VI and Mary. She, too, succeeded —and with the hearty goodwill of nearly all her subjects.

Mary had left the royal treasury deeply in debt. Yet Elizabeth succeeded in paying off all arrears and meeting new expenditure for defence and for the court. The royal income rose. England became immensely richer and more prosperous than ever before. Foreign trade increased by leaps and bounds. Home industries flourished and were stimulated by new arrivals from abroad, because England was a safe asylum for the craftsmen whom Philip was driving from the Netherlands, to his own great loss and his rival's gain.

English commercial life had been slowly emerging from mediæval ways throughout the fifteenth century. With the beginning of the sixteenth the rate of emergence had greatly quickened. The soil-bound peasant who produced enough food for his family from his thirty acres was being gradually replaced by the well-to-do yeoman who tilled a hundred acres and upwards. Such holdings produced a substantial surplus for the market. This increased the national wealth, which, in its turn, increased both home and foreign trade. The peasant merely raised a little wheat and barley, kept a cow, and perhaps some sheep. The yeoman or tenant farmer had sheep enough for the wool trade besides some butter, cheese, and meat for the nearest growing town. He began to 'garnish his cupboards with pewter and his joined beds with tapestry and silk hangings, and his tables with carpets and fine napery.' He could even feast his neighbors and servants after shearing day with new-fangled foreign luxuries like dates, mace, raisins, currants, and sugar.

But Elizabethan society presented striking contrasts. In parts of England, the practice of engrossing and enclosing holdings was increasing, as sheep-raising became more profitable than farming. The tenants thus dispossessed either swelled the ranks of the vagabonds who infested

the highways or sought their livelihood at sea or in
London, which provided the two best openings
for adventurous young men. The smaller pro-
vincial towns afforded them little opportunity,
for there the trades were largely in the hands of
close corporations descended from the mediæval
craft guilds. These were eventually to be swept
away by the general trend of business. Their
dissolution had indeed already begun; for smart
village craftsmen were even then forming the
new industrial settlements from which most of
the great manufacturing towns of England have
sprung. Camden the historian found Birming-
ham full of ringing anvils, Sheffield 'a town of
great name for the smiths therein,' Leeds renowned
for cloth, and Manchester already a sort of cotton-
opolis, though the 'cottons' of those days were
still made of wool.

There was a wages question then as now. There
were demands for a minimum living wage. The
influx of gold and silver from America had sent
all prices soaring. Meat became almost pro-
hibitive for the 'submerged tenth' — there was a
rapidly submerging tenth. Beef rose from one
cent a pound in the forties to four in 1588, the
year of the Armada. How would the lowest

paid of craftsmen fare on twelve cents a day, with butter at ten cents a pound? Efforts were made, again and again, to readjust the ratio between prices and wages. But, as a rule, prices increased much faster than wages.

All these things — the increase of surplus hands, the high cost of living, grievances about wages and interest — tended to make the farms and workshops of England recruiting-grounds for the sea; and the young men would strike out for themselves as freighters, traders, privateers, or downright pirates, lured by the dazzling chance of great and sudden wealth.

'The gamble of it' was as potent then as now, probably more potent still. It was an age of wild speculation accompanied by all the usual evils that follow frenzied ways. It was also an age of monopoly. Both monopoly and specula-tion sent recruits into the sea-dog ranks. Eliza-beth would grant, say, to Sir Walter Raleigh, the monopoly of sweet wines. Raleigh would naturally want as much sweet wine imported as England could be induced to swallow. So, too, would Elizabeth, who got the duty. Crews would be wanted for the monopolistic ships. They would also be wanted for 'free-trading' vessels, that is, for the ships of the smugglers who underbid, undersold, and tried to overreach the monopolist, who represented law, though not quite justice. But speculation ran to greater extremes than either monopoly or smuggling. Shakespeare's 'Putter-out of five for one' was a typical Elizabethan speculator exploiting the riskiest form of sea-dog trade for all — and sometimes for more than all — that it was worth. A merchant-adventurer would pay a capitalist, say, a thousand pounds as a premium to be forfeited if his ship should be lost, but to be repaid by the capitalist fivefold to the merchant if it returned. Incredible as it may seem to us, there were shrewd money-lenders always ready for this sort of deal in life — or life-and-death — insurance: an eloquent testimony to the risks encountered in sailing unknown seas in the midst of well-known dangers.

Marine insurance of the regular kind was, of course, a very different thing. It was already of immemorial age, going back certainly to mediæval and probably to very ancient times. All forms of insurance on land are mere mushrooms by comparison. Lloyd's had not been heard of. But there were plenty of smart Elizabethan underwriters already practising the general principles which were to be formally adopted two hundred years later, in 1779, at Lloyd's Coffee House. A policy taken out on the *Tiger* immortalized by Shakespeare would serve as a model still. And what makes it all the more interesting is that the Elizabethan underwriters calculated the *Tiger's* chances at the very spot where the association known as Lloyd's transacts its business to-day, the Royal Exchange in London. This, in turn, brings Elizabeth herself upon the scene; for when she visited the Exchange, which Sir Thomas Gresham had built to let the merchants do their street work under cover, she immediately grasped its full significance and 'caused it by an Herald and a Trumpet to be proclaimed The Royal Exchange,' the name it bears to-day. An Elizabethan might well be astonished by what he would see at any modern Lloyd's. Yet he would find the same essentials; for the British Lloyd's, like most of its foreign imitators, is not a gigantic insurance company at all, but an association of cautiously elected members who carry on their completely independent private business in daily touch with each other — precisely as Elizabethans did. Lloyd's method differs wholly from ordi-

QUEEN ELIZABETH

Painting attributed to Federigo Zucchero. In the National Portrait Gallery, London, England.

QUEEN ELIZABETH

Painting attributed to Federigo Zucchero. In the National Portrait Gallery, London, England.

nary insurance. Instead of insuring vessel and
cargo with a single company or man the owner
puts his case before Lloyd's, and any member can
then write his name underneath for any reasonable part of the risk. The modern 'underwriter,'
all the world over, is the direct descendant of the
Elizabethan who wrote his name under the conditions of a given risk at sea.

Joint-stock companies were in one sense old
when Elizabethan men of business were young.
But the Elizabethans developed them enormously.
'Going shares' was doubtless prehistoric. It
certainly was ancient, mediæval, and Elizabethan.
But those who formerly went shares generally
knew each other and something of the business
too. The favorite number of total shares was
just sixteen. There were sixteen land-shares in
a Celtic household, sixteen shares in Scottish
vessels not individually owned, sixteen shares in
the theatre by which Shakespeare 'made his pile.'
But sixteenths, and even hundredths, were put
out of date when speculation on the grander
scale began and the area of investment grew.
The New River Company, for supplying London
with water, had only a few shares then, as it continued to have down to our own day, when they

stood at over a thousand times par. The Ulster
'Plantation' in Ireland was more remote and
appealed to more investors and on wider grounds
— sentimental grounds, both good and bad,
included. The Virginia 'Plantation' was still
more remote and risky and appealed to an ever-
increasing number of the speculating public.
Many an investor put money on America in much
the same way as a factory hand to-day puts
money on a horse he has never seen or has never
heard of otherwise than as something out of which
a lot of easy money can be made provided luck
holds good.

The modern prospectus was also in full career
under Elizabeth, who probably had a hand in
concocting some of the most important specimens.
Lord Bacon wrote one describing the advantages
of the Newfoundland fisheries in terms which no
promoter of the present day could better. Every
type of prospectus was tried on the investing
public, some genuine, many doubtful, others as
outrageous in their impositions on human credulity
as anything produced in our own times. The
company-promoter was abroad, in London, on
'Change, and at court. What with royal favor,
social prestige, general prosperity, the new na-

tional eagerness to find vent for surplus commodities, and, above all, the spirit of speculation
fanned into flame by the real and fabled wonders
of America, what with all this the investing public
could take its choice of 'going the limit' in a hundred different and most alluring ways. England
was surprised at her own investing wealth. The
East India Company raised eight million dollars
with ease from a thousand shareholders and paid
a first dividend of $87\frac{1}{2}$ per cent. Spices, pearls,
and silks came pouring into London; and English
goods found vent increasingly abroad.

Vastly expanding business opportunities of
course produced the spirit of the trust — and of
very much the same sort of trust that Americans
think so ultra-modern now. Monopolies granted
by the Crown and the volcanic forces of widespread
speculation prevented some of the abuses of the
trust. But there were Elizabethan trusts, for
all that, though many a promising scheme fell
through. The Feltmakers' Hat Trust is a case
in point. They proposed buying up all the hats
in the market so as to oblige all dealers to depend
upon one central warehouse. Of course they
issued a prospectus showing how everyone concerned would benefit by this benevolent plan.

Ben Jonson and other playwrights were quick to seize the salient absurdities of such an advertisement. In *The Staple of News* Jonson proposed a News Trust to collect all the news of the world, corner it, classify it into authentic, apocryphal, barber's gossip, and so forth, and then sell it, for the sole benefit of the consumer, in lengths to suit all purchasers. In *The Devil is an Ass* he is a little more outspoken.

> We'll take in citizens, commoners, and aldermen
> To bear the charge, and blow them off again
> Like so many dead flies. . . .

This was exactly what was at that very moment being done in the case of the Alum Trust. All the leading characters of much more modern times were there already; Fitzdottrell, ready to sell his estates in order to become His Grace the Duke of Drown'dland, Gilthead, the London moneylender who 'lives by finding fools,' and My Lady Tailbush, who pulls the social wires at court. And so the game went on, usually with the result explained by Shakespeare's fisherman in *Pericles:*

> 'I marvel how the fishes live in the sea'—
> 'Why, as men do a-land: the great ones eat up the
> little ones.'

The Newcastle coal trade grew into something very like a modern American trust with the additional advantage of an authorized government monopoly so long as the agreed-upon duty was paid. Then there was the Starch Monopoly, a very profitable one because starch was a new delight which soon enabled Elizabethan fops to wear ruffed collars big enough to make their heads — as one irreverent satirist exclaimed — 'look like John Baptist's on a platter.'

But America? Could not America defeat the machinations of all monopolies and other trusts? Wasn't America the land of actual gold and silver where there was plenty of room for everyone? There soon grew up a wild belief that you could tap America for precious metals almost as its Indians tapped maple trees for sugar. The 'Mountains of Bright Stones' were surely there. Peru and Mexico were nothing to these. Only find them, and 'get-rich-quick' would be the order of the day for every true adventurer. These mountains moved about in men's imaginations and on prospectors' maps, always ahead of the latest pioneer, somewhere behind the Back of Beyond. They and their glamour died hard. Even that staid geographer of a later day, Thos.

5

Jeffreys, added to his standard atlas of America, in 1760, this item of information on the Far Northwest: *Hereabouts are supposed to be the Mountains of Bright Stones mentioned in the Map of ye Indian Ochagach.*

Speculation of the wildcat kind was bad. But it was the seamy side of a praiseworthy spirit of enterprise. Monopoly seems worse than speculation. And so, in many ways, it was. But we must judge it by the custom of its age. It was often unjust and generally obstructive. But it did what neither the national government nor joint-stock companies had yet learnt to do. Monopoly went by court favor, and its rights were often scandalously let and sometimes sublet as well. But, on the whole, the Queen, the court, and the country really meant business, and monopolists had either to deliver the goods or get out. Monopolists sold dispensations from unworkable laws, which was sometimes a good thing and sometimes a bad. They sold licenses for indulgence in forbidden pleasures, not often harmless. They thought out and collected all kinds of indirect taxation and had to face all the troubles that confront the framers of a tariff policy to-day. Most of all, however, in a rough-and-ready way they set a sort of Civil Service going. They served as Boards of Trade, Departments of the Interior, Customs, Inland Revenue, and so forth. What Crown and Parliament either could not or would not do was farmed out to monopolists. Like speculation the system worked both ways, and frequently for evil. But, like the British constitution, though on a lower plane, it worked.

A monopoly at home — like those which we have been considering — was endurable because it was a working compromise that suited existing circumstances more or less, and that could be either mended or ended as time went on. But a general foreign monopoly — like Spain's monopoly of America—was quite unendurable. Could Spain not only hold what she had discovered and was exploiting but also extend her sphere of influence over what she had not discovered? Spain said Yes. England said No. The Spaniards looked for tribute. The English looked for trade. In government, in religion, in business, in everything, the two great rivals were irreconcilably opposed. Thus the lists were set; and sea-dog battles followed.

Elizabeth was an exceedingly able woman of business and was practically president of all the great joint-stock companies engaged in oversea trade. Wherever a cargo could be bought or sold there went an English ship to buy or sell it. Whenever the authorities in foreign parts tried discrimination against English men or English goods, the English sea-dogs growled and showed their teeth. And if the foreigners persisted, the sea-dogs bit them.

Elizabeth was extravagant at court; but not without state motives for at least a part of her extravagance. A brilliant court attracted the upper classes into the orbit of the Crown while it impressed the whole country with the sovereign's power. Courtiers favored with monopolies had to spend their earnings when the state was threatened. And might not the Queen's vast profusion of jewelry be turned to account at a pinch? Elizabeth could not afford to be generous when she was young. She grew to be stingy when she was old. But she saved the state by sound finance as well as by arms in spite of all her pomps and vanities. She had three thousand dresses, and gorgeous ones at that, during the course of her reign. Her bathroom was wainscoted with Venetian mirrors so that she could see 'nine-and-ninety' reflections of her very comely person as she dipped and splashed or dried her royal skin. She set a hot pace for all the votaries of dress to follow. All kinds of fashions came in from abroad with the rush of new-found wealth; and so, instead of being sanely beautiful, they soon became insanely bizarre. 'An Englishman,' says Harrison, 'endeavouring to write of our attire, gave over his travail, and only drew the picture of a naked man, since he could find no kind of garment that could please him any whiles together.

I am an English man and naked I stand here,
Musing in my mind what raiment I shall were;
For now I will were this, and now I will were that;
And now I will were I cannot tell what.

Except you see a dog in a doublet you shall not see any so disguised as are my countrymen of England. Women also do far exceed the lightness of our men. What shall I say of their galligascons to bear out their attire and make it fit plum round?' But the wives of 'citizens and burgesses,' like all *nouveaux riches*, were still more bizarre than the courtiers. 'They cannot tell when or how to make an end, being women in whom all kind of curiosity is to be seen in far greater measure than in women of higher calling.

I might name hues devised for the nonce, ver d'oye 'twixt green and yellow, peas-porridge tawny, popinjay blue, and the Devil-in-the-head.'

Yet all this crude absurdity, 'from the courtier to the carter,' was the glass reflecting the constantly increasing sea-borne trade, ever pushing farther afield under the stimulus and protection of the sea-dogs. And the Queen took precious good care that it all paid toll to her treasury through the customs, so that she could have more money to build more ships. And if her courtiers did stuff their breeches out with sawdust, she took equally good care that each fighting man among them donned his uniform and raised his troops or fitted out his ships when the time was ripe for action.

CHAPTER V

HAWKINS AND THE FIGHTING TRADERS

SAID Francis I of France to Charles V, King of Spain: 'Your Majesty and the King of Portugal have divided the world between you, offering no part of it to me. Show me, I pray you, the will of our father Adam, so that I may see if he has really made you his only universal heirs!' Then Francis sent out the Italian navigator Verrazano, who first explored the coast from Florida to Newfoundland. Afterwards Jacques Cartier discovered the St. Lawrence; Frenchmen took Havana twice, plundered the Spanish treasure-ships, and tried to found colonies — Catholic in Canada, Protestant in Florida and Brazil.

Thus, at the time when Elizabeth ascended the throne of England in 1558, there was a long-established New Spain extending over Mexico, the West Indies, and most of South America;

a small New Portugal confined to part of Brazil; and a shadowy New France running vaguely inland from the Gulf of St. Lawrence, nowhere effectively occupied, and mostly overlapping prior English claims based on the discoveries of the Cabots.

England and France had often been enemies. England and Spain had just been allied in a war against France as well as by the marriage of Philip and Mary. William Hawkins had traded with Portuguese Brazil under Henry VIII, as the Southampton merchants were to do later on. English merchants lived in Lisbon and Cadiz; a few were even settled in New Spain; and a friendly Spaniard had been so delighted by the prospective union of the English with the Spanish crown that he had given the name of Londres (London) to a new settlement in the Argentine Andes.

Presently, however, Elizabethan England began to part company with Spain, to become more anti-Papal, to sympathize with Huguenots and other heretics, and, like Francis I, to wonder why an immense new world should be nothing but New Spain. Besides, Englishmen knew what the rest of Europe knew, that the discovery of

Potosi had put out of business nearly all the Old-World silver mines, and that the Burgundian Ass (as Spanish treasure-mules were called, from Charles's love of Burgundy) had enabled Spain to make conquests, impose her will on her neighbors, and keep paid spies in every foreign court, the English court included. Londoners had seen Spanish gold and silver paraded through the streets when Philip married Mary — '27 chests of bullion, 99 horseloads + 2 cartloads of gold and silver coin, and 97 boxes full of silver bars!' Moreover, the Holy Inquisition was making Spanish seaports pretty hot for heretics. In 1562, twenty-six English subjects were burnt alive in Spain itself. Ten times as many were in prison. No wonder sea-dogs were straining at the leash.

Neither Philip nor Elizabeth wanted war just then, though each enjoyed a thrust at the other by any kind of fighting short of that, and though each winked at all kinds of armed trade, such as privateering and even downright piracy. The English and Spanish merchants had commercial connections going back for centuries; and business men on both sides were always ready to do a good stroke for themselves.

This was the state of affairs in 1562 when young

John Hawkins, son of 'Olde Master William,' went into the slave trade with New Spain. Except for the fact that both Portugal and Spain allowed no trade with their oversea possessions in any ships but their own, the circumstances appeared to favor his enterprise. The American Indians were withering away before the atrocious cruelties of the Portuguese and Spaniards, being either killed in battle, used up in merciless slavery, or driven off to alien wilds. Already the Portuguese had commenced to import negroes from their West African possessions, both for themselves and for trade with the Spaniards, who had none. Brazil prospered beyond expectation and absorbed all the blacks that Portuguese shipping could supply. The Spaniards had no spare tonnage at the time.

John Hawkins, aged thirty, had made several trips to the Canaries. He now formed a joint-stock company to trade with the Spaniards farther off. Two Lord Mayors of London and the Treasurer of the Royal Navy were among the subscribers. Three small vessels, with only two hundred and sixty tons between them, formed the flotilla. The crews numbered just a hundred men. 'At Teneriffe he received friendly treatment. From thence he passed to Sierra Leona, where he stayed a good time, and got into his possession, partly by the sword and partly by other means, to the number of 300 Negroes at the least, besides other merchandises. . . . With this prey he sailed over the ocean sea unto the island of Hispaniola [Hayti] . . . and here he had reasonable utterance [sale] of his English commodities, as also of some part of his Negroes, trusting the Spaniards no further than that by his own strength he was able still to master them.' At 'Monte Christi, another port on the north side of Hispaniola . . . he made vent of [sold] the whole number of his Negroes, for which he received by way of exchange such a quantity of merchandise that he did not only lade his own three ships with hides, ginger, sugars, and some quantity of pearls, but he freighted also two other hulks with hides and other like commodities, which he sent into Spain,' where both hulks and hides were confiscated as being contraband.

Nothing daunted, he was off again in 1564 with four ships and a hundred and seventy men. This time Elizabeth herself took shares and lent the *Jesus of Lubeck*, a vessel of seven hundred tons which Henry VIII had bought for the navy.

Nobody questioned slavery in those days. The great Spanish missionary Las Casas denounced the Spanish atrocities against the Indians. But he thought negroes, who could be domesticated, would do as substitutes for Indians, who could not be domesticated. The Indians withered at the white man's touch. The negroes, if properly treated, throve, and were safer than among their enemies at home. Such was the argument for slavery; and it was true so far as it went. The argument against, on the score of ill treatment, was only gradually heard. On the score of general human rights it was never heard at all.

'At departing, in cutting the foresail lashings a marvellous misfortune happened to one of the officers in the ship, who by the pulley of the sheet was slain out of hand.' Hawkins 'appointed all the masters of his ships an Order for the keeping of good company in this manner: — The small ships to be always ahead and aweather of the *Jesus*, and to speak twice a-day with the *Jesus* at least. . . . If the weather be extreme, that the small ships cannot keep company with the *Jesus*, then all to keep company with the *Solomon*. . . . If any happen to any misfortune, then to show two lights, and to shoot off a piece

IOANNES HAVKINS

Aduancement by diligence.

Grauure Andersen-Lamb.Co.N.Y.

Qui Vicit tobiens in Fructis classibus Hos
Ille Vagis HAVKINS Vitam relliquit in Vndis

of ordnance. If any lose company and come in sight again, to make three yaws [zigzags in their course] and strike the mizzen three times. SERVE GOD DAILY. LOVE ONE ANOTHER. PRESERVE YOUR VICTUALS. BEWARE OF FIRE, AND KEEP GOOD COMPANY.'

John Sparke, the chronicler of this second voyage, was full of curiosity over every strange sight he met with. He was also blessed with the pen of a ready writer. So we get a story that is more vivacious than Hakluyt's retelling of the first voyage or Hawkins's own account of the third. Sparke saw for the first time in his life negroes, Caribs, Indians, alligators, flying-fish, flamingoes, pelicans, and many other strange sights. Having been told that Florida was full of unicorns he at once concluded that it must also be full of lions; for how could the one kind exist without the other kind to balance it? Sparke was a soldier who never found his sea legs. But his diary, besides its other merits, is particularly interesting as being the first account of America ever written by an English eye-witness.

Hawkins made for Teneriffe in the Canaries, off the west of Africa. There, to everybody's great 'amaze,' the Spaniards 'appeared levelling of bases [small portable cannon] and arquebuses, with divers others, to the number of fourscore, with halberds, pikes, swords, and targets.' But when it was found that Hawkins had been taken for a privateer, and when it is remembered that four hundred privateering vessels — English and Huguenot — had captured seven hundred Spanish prizes during the previous summer of 1563, there was and is less cause for 'amaze.' Once explanations had been made, 'Peter de Ponte gave Master Hawkins as gentle entertainment as if he had been his own brother.' Peter was a trader with a great eye for the main chance.

Sparke was lost in wonder over the famous Arbol Santo tree of Ferro, 'by the dropping whereof the inhabitants and cattle are satisfied with water, for other water they have none on the island.' This is not quite the traveller's tale it appears to be. There are three springs on the island of Teneriffe. But water is scarce, and the Arbol Santo, a sort of gigantic laurel standing alone on a rocky ledge, did actually supply two cisterns, one for men and the other for cattle. The morning mist condensing on the innumerable smooth leaves ran off and was caught in suitable conduits.

In Africa Hawkins took many 'Sapies which do inhabit about Rio Grande [now the Jeba River] which do jag their flesh, both legs, arms, and bodies as workmanlike as a jerkin-maker with us pinketh a jerkin.' It is a nice question whether these Sapies gained or lost by becoming slaves to white men; for they were already slaves to black conquerors who used them as meat with the vegetables they forced them to raise. The Sapies were sleek pacifists who found too late that the warlike Samboses, who inhabited the neighboring desert, were not to be denied.

'In the island of Sambula we found almadies or canoas, which are made of one piece of wood, digged out like a trough, but of a good proportion, being about eight yards long and one in breadth, having a beak-head and a stern very proportionably made, and on the outside artificially carved, and painted red and blue.' Neither *almadie* nor *canoa* is, of course, an African word. One is Arabic for a cradle (*el-mahd*); the other, from which we get *canoe*, is what the natives told Columbus they called their dugouts; and dugout canoes are very like primitive cradles. Thus Sparke was the first man to record in English, from actual experience, the aboriginal craft whose

name, both East and West, was suggested to
primeval man by the idea of his being literally
'rocked in the cradle of the deep.'

Hawkins did not have it all his own way with
the negroes, by whom he once lost seven of his
own men killed and twenty-seven wounded. 'But
the captain in a singular wise manner carried
himself with countenance very cheerful outwardly,
although inwardly his heart was broken in pieces
for it; done to this end, that the Portugals, being
with him, should not presume to resist against
him.' After losing five more men, who were
eaten by sharks, Hawkins shaped his course
westward with a good cargo of negroes and 'other
merchandises.' 'Contrary winds and some tor-
nados happened to us very ill. But the Almighty
God, who never suffereth His elect to perish, sent
us the ordinary Breeze, which never left us till
we came to an island of the Cannibals' (Caribs of
Dominica), who, by the by, had just eaten a
shipload of Spaniards.

Hawkins found the Spanish officials determined
to make a show of resisting unauthorized trade.
But when 'he prepared 100 men well armed with
bows, arrows, arquebuses, and pikes, with which
he marched townwards,' the officials let the sale

of blacks go on. Hawkins was particularly anxious to get rid of his 'lean negroes,' who might die in his hands and become a dead loss; so he used the 'gunboat argument' to good effect. Sparke kept his eyes open for side-shows and was delighted with the alligators, which he called crocodiles, perhaps for the sake of the crocodile tears. 'His nature is to cry and sob like a Christian to provoke his prey to come to him; and thereupon came this proverb, that is applied unto women when they weep, *lachrymæ crocodili*.'

From the West Indies Hawkins made for Florida, which was then an object of exceptional desire among adventurous Englishmen. De Soto, one of Pizarro's lieutenants, had annexed it to Spain and, in 1539, had started off inland to discover the supposed Peru of North America. Three years later he had died while descending the valley of the Mississippi. Six years later again, the first Spanish missionary in Florida 'taking upon him to persuade the people to subjection, was by them taken, and his skin cruelly pulled over his ears, and his flesh eaten.' Hawkins's men had fair warning on the way; for 'they, being ashore, found a dead man, dried in a manner whole, with other heads and bodies of men,' apparently smoked

6

like hams. 'But to return to our purpose,' adds
the indefatigable Sparke, 'the captain in the ship's
pinnace sailed along the shore and went into every
creek, speaking with divers of the *Floridians*, because he would understand where the Frenchmen
inhabited.' Finally he found them 'in the river
of *May* [now St. John's River] and standing in
30 degrees and better.' There was 'great store
of maize and mill, and grapes of great bigness.
Also deer great plenty, which came upon the
sands before them.'

So here were the three rivals overlapping again
— the annexing Spaniards, the would-be colonizing French, and the persistently trading English.
There were, however, no Spaniards about at that
time. This was the second Huguenot colony in
Florida. René de Laudonnière had founded it
in 1564. The first one, founded two years earlier
by Jean Ribaut, had failed and Ribaut's men had
deserted the place. They had started for home
in 1563, had suffered terrible hardships, had been
picked up by an English vessel, and taken, some
to France and some to England, where the court
was all agog about the wealth of Florida. People
said there were mines so bright with jewels that
they had to be approached at night lest the flash-

ing light should strike men blind. Florida became proverbial; and Elizabethan wits made
endless fun of it. *Stolida*, or the land of fools,
and *Sordida*, or the land of muck-worms, were
some of their *jeux d'esprit*. Everyone was 'bound
for Florida,' whether he meant to go there or not,
despite Spanish spheres of influence, the native
cannibals, and pirates by the way.

Hawkins, on the contrary, did not profess to
be bound for Florida. Nevertheless he arrived
there, and probably had intended to do so from
the first, for he took with him a Frenchman who
had been in Ribaut's colony two years before, and
Sparke significantly says that 'the land is more
than any [one] king Christian is able to inhabit.'
However this may be, Hawkins found the second
French colony as well as 'a French ship of fourscore ton, and two pinnaces of fifteen ton apiece
by her . . . and a fort, in which their captain
Monsieur Laudonnière was, with certain soldiers
therein.' The colony had not been a success.
Nor is this to be wondered at when we remember
that most of the 'certain soldiers' were ex-pirates,
who wanted gold, and 'who would not take the
pains so much as to fish in the river before their
doors, but would have all things put in their

mouths.' Eighty of the original two hundred
'went a-roving' to the West Indies, 'where they
spoiled the Spaniards . . . and were of such
haughty stomachs that they thought their force
to be such that no man durst meddle with them.
. . . But God . . . did indurate their hearts in
such sort that they lingered so long that a [Span-
ish] ship and galliasse being made out of St.
Domingo . . . took twenty of them, whereof the
most part were hanged . . . and twenty-five
escaped . . . to Florida, where . . . they were
put into prison [by Laudonnière, against whom
they had mutinied] and . . . four of the chiefest
being condemned, at the request of the soldiers
did pass the arquebusers, and then were hanged
upon a gibbet.' Sparke got the delightful ex-
pression 'at the request of the soldiers did pass
the arquebusers' from a 'very polite' Frenchman.
Could any one tell you more politely, in mistrans-
lated language, how to stand up and be shot?

Sparke was greatly taken with the unknown
art of smoking. 'The Floridians . . . have an
herb dried, who, with a cane and an earthen cup
in the end, with fire and the dried herbs put together, do suck through the cane the smoke
thereof, which smoke satisfieth their hunger,

and therewith they live four or five days without meat or drink. And this all the Frenchmen used for this purpose; yet do they hold opinion withal that it causeth water and steam to void from their stomachs.' The other 'commodities of the land' were 'more than are yet known to any man.' But Hawkins was bent on trade, not colonizing. He sold the *Tiger*, a barque of fifty tons, to Laudonnière for seven hundred crowns and sailed north on the first voyage ever made along the coast of the United States by an all-English crew. Turning east off Newfoundland 'with a good large wind, the 20 September [1565] we came to Padstow, in Cornwall, God be thanked! in safety, with the loss of twenty persons in all the voyage, and with great profit to the venturers, as also to the whole realm, in bringing home both gold, silver, pearls, and other jewels great store. His name, therefore, be praised for evermore. Amen.'

Hawkins was now a rich man, a favorite at court, and quite the rage in London. The Queen was very gracious and granted him the well-known coat of arms with the crest of 'a demi-Moor, bound and captive' in honor of the great new English slave trade. The Spanish ambassador met him at court and asked him to dinner, where, over the wine, Hawkins assured him that he was going out again next year. Meanwhile, however, the famous Captain-General of the Indian trade, Don Pedro Menendez de Aviles, the best naval officer that Spain perhaps has ever had, swooped down on the French in Florida, killed them all, and built the fort of St. Augustine to guard the 'Mountains of Bright Stones' somewhere in the hinterland. News of this slaughter soon arrived at Madrid, whence orders presently went out to have an eye on Hawkins, whom Spanish officials thenceforth regarded as the leading interloper in New Spain.

Nevertheless Hawkins set out on his third and very 'troublesome' voyage in 1567, backed by all his old and many new supporters, and with a flotilla of six vessels, the *Jesus*, the *Minion* (which then meant darling), the *William and John*, the *Judith*, the *Angel*, and the *Swallow*. This was the voyage that began those twenty years of sea-dog fighting which rose to their zenith in the battle against the Armada; and with this voyage Drake himself steps on to the stage as captain of the *Judith*.

There had been a hitch in 1566, for the Spanish ambassador had reported Hawkins's after-dinner speech to his king. Philip had protested to Elizabeth, and Elizabeth had consulted with Cecil, afterwards 'the great Lord Burleigh,' ancestor of the Marquis of Salisbury, British Prime Minister during the Spanish-American War of 1898. The result was that orders went down to Plymouth stopping Hawkins and binding him over, in a bond of five hundred pounds, to keep the peace with Her Majesty's right good friend King Philip of Spain. But in 1567 times had changed again, and Hawkins sailed with colors flying, for Elizabeth was now as ready to hurt Philip as he was to hurt her, provided always that open war was carefully avoided.

But this time things went wrong from the first. A tremendous autumnal storm scattered the ships. Then the first negroes that Hawkins tried to 'snare' proved to be like that other kind of prey of which the sarcastic Frenchman wrote: 'This animal is very wicked; when you attack it, it defends itself.' The 'envenomed arrows' of the negroes worked the mischief. 'There hardly escaped any that had blood drawn of them, but died in strange sort, with their mouths shut some ten days before they died.' Hawkins himself was wounded, but, 'thanks be to God,' escaped the lockjaw. After this the English took sides in a native war and captured '250 persons, men, women, and children,' while their friend the King captured '600 prisoners, whereof we hoped to have had our choice. But the negro, in which nation is seldom or never found truth, that night removed his camp and prisoners, so that we were fain to content ourselves with those few we had gotten ourselves.'

However, with 'between 400 and 500 negroes,' Hawkins crossed over from Africa to the West Indies and 'coasted from place to place, making our traffic with the Spaniards as we might, somewhat hardly, because the King had straitly commanded all his governors by no means to suffer any trade to be made with us. Notwithstanding, we had reasonable trade, and courteous entertainment' for a good part of the way. In Rio de la Hacha the Spaniards received the English with a volley that killed a couple of men, whereupon the English smashed in the gates, while the Spaniards retired. But, after this little bit of punctilio, trade went on under cover of night so briskly that two hundred negroes were sold at good prices. From there to Cartagena 'the inhabitants were glad of us and traded willingly,' supply being short and demand extra high.

Then came a real rebuff from the governor of Cartagena, followed by a terrific storm 'which so beat the *Jesus* that we cut down all her higher buildings' (deck superstructures). Then the course was shaped for Florida. But a new storm drove the battered flotilla back to 'the port which serveth the city of Mexico, called St. John de Ulua,' the modern Vera Cruz. The historic Vera Cruz was fifteen miles north of this harbor. Here 'thinking us to be the fleet of Spain, the chief officers of the country came aboard us. Which, being deceived of their expectation, were greatly dismayed; but . . . when they saw our demand was nothing but victuals, were recomforted. I [for it is Hawkins's own story] found in the same port 12 ships which had in them by report £200,000 in gold and silver, all which, being in my possession [*i. e.*, at my mercy] with the King's Island . . . I set at liberty.'

What was to be done? Hawkins had a hundred negroes still to sell. But it was four hundred miles to Mexico City and back again; and a new Spanish viceroy was aboard the big Spanish fleet that was daily expected to arrive in this very port. If a permit to sell came back from the capital in time, well and good. If no more than time to replenish stores was allowed, good enough, despite the loss of sales. But what if the Spanish fleet arrived? The 'King's Island' was a low little reef right in the mouth of the harbor, which it all but barred. Moreover, no vessel could live through a northerly gale inside the harbor — the only one on that coast — unless securely moored to the island itself. Consequently whoever held the island commanded the situation altogether.

There was not much time for consultation; for the very next morning 'we saw open of the haven 13 great ships, the fleet of Spain.' It was a terrible predicament. *'Now,* said I, *I am in two dangers, and forced to receive the one of them.* . . . Either I must have kept out the fleet, which, with God's help, I was very well able to do, or else suffer them to enter with their accustomed treason. . . . If I had kept them out, then there had been present shipwreck of all that fleet, which amounted in value to six millions, which was in value of our money £1,800,000, which I considered I was not able to answer, fearing the Queen's Majesty's indignation. . . . Thus with myself revolving the doubts, I thought better to abide the jut of the uncertainty than of the certainty.' So, after conditions had been agreed upon and hostages exchanged, the thirteen Spanish ships sailed in. The little island remained in English hands; and the Spaniards were profuse in promises.

But, having secretly made their preparations, the Spaniards, who were in overwhelming numbers, suddenly set upon the English by land and sea. Every Englishman ashore was killed, except a few who got off in a boat to the *Jesus*. The *Jesus* and the *Minion* cut their headfasts, hauled clear by their sternfasts, drove back the boarding parties, and engaged the Spanish fleet at about a hundred yards. Within an hour the Spanish flagship and another were sunk, a third vessel was burning furiously, fore and aft, while every English deck was clear of enemies. But the Spaniards had swarmed on to the island from all sides and were firing into the English hulls at only a few feet from the cannon's mouth. Hawkins was cool as ever. Calling for a tankard of beer he drank to the health of the gunners, who accounted for most of the five hundred and forty men killed on the Spanish side. 'Stand by your

ordnance lustily,' he cried, as he put the tankard
down and a round shot sent it flying. 'God hath
delivered me,' he added, 'and so will He deliver
you from these traitors and villains.'

The masts of the *Jesus* went by the board and
her old, strained timbers splintered, loosened up,
and were stove in under the storm of cannon
balls. Hawkins then gave the order to abandon
ship after taking out what stores they could and
changing her berth so that she would shield the
little *Minion*. But while this desperate manœuvre
was being executed down came two fire-ships.
Some of the *Minion's* crew then lost their heads
and made sail so quickly that Hawkins himself
was nearly left behind.

The only two English vessels that escaped were
the *Minion* and the *Judith*. When nothing else
was left to do, Hawkins shouted to Drake to lay
the *Judith* aboard the *Minion*, take in all the men
and stores he could, and put to sea. Drake,
then only twenty-three, did this with consummate
skill. Hawkins followed some time after and
anchored just out of range. But Drake had
already gained an offing that caused the two little
vessels to part company in the night, during which
a whole gale from the north sprang up, threatening

to put the *Judith* on a lee shore. Drake therefore fought his way to windward; and, seeing no
one when the gale abated, and having barely
enough stores to make a friendly land, sailed
straight home. Hawkins reported the *Judith*,
without mentioning Drake's name, as 'forsaking'
the *Minion*. But no other witness thought
Drake to blame.

Hawkins himself rode out the gale under the
lee of a little island, then beat about for two weeks
of increasing misery, when 'hides were thought
very good meat, and rats, cats, mice, and dogs,
parrots and monkeys that were got at great price,
none escaped.' The *Minion* was of three hundred
tons; and so was insufferably overcrowded with
three hundred men, two hundred English and one
hundred negroes. Drake's little *Judith*, of only
fifty tons, could have given no relief, as she was
herself overfull. Hawkins asked all the men
who preferred to take their chance on land to
get round the foremast and all those who wanted
to remain afloat to get round the mizzen. About
a hundred chose one course and a hundred the
other. The landing took place about a hundred
and fifty miles south of the Rio Grande. The
shore party nearly all died. But three lived to

write of their adventures. David Ingram, following Indian trails all round the Gulf of Mexico and up the Atlantic seaboard, came out where St. John, New Brunswick, stands now, was picked up by a passing Frenchman, and so got safely home. Job Hortop and Miles Philips were caught by the Spaniards and sent back to Mexico. Philips escaped to England fourteen years later. But Hortop was sent to Spain, where he served twelve years as a galley-slave and ten as a servant before he contrived to get aboard an English vessel.

The ten Spanish hostages were found safe and sound aboard the *Jesus;* though, by all the rules of war, Hawkins would have been amply justified in killing them. The English hostages were kept fast prisoners. 'If all the miseries of this sorrowful voyage,' says Hawkins's report, 'should be perfectly written, there should need a painful man with his pen, and as great a time as he had that wrote the lives and deaths of martyrs.'

Thus, in complete disaster, ended that third voyage to New Spain on which so many hopes were set. And with this disastrous end began those twenty years of sea-dog rage which found their satisfaction against the Great Armada.

CHAPTER VI

DRAKE'S BEGINNING

WE must now turn back for a moment to 1545, the year in which the Old World, after the discovery of the mines of Potosi, first awoke to the illimitable riches of the New; the year in which King Henry assembled his epoch-making fleet; the year, too, in which the British National Anthem was, so to say, born at sea, when the parole throughout the waiting fleet was *God save the King!* and the answering countersign was *Long to reign over us!*

In the same year, at Crowndale by Tavistock in Devon, was born Francis Drake, greatest of sea-dogs and first of modern admirals. His father, Edmund Drake, was a skipper in modest circumstances. But from time immemorial there had been Drakes all round the countryside of Tavistock and the family name stood high. Francis was called after his godfather, Francis

Russell, son and heir of Henry's right-hand re-
forming peer, Lord Russell, progenitor of the
Dukes of Bedford down to the present day.

Though fortune thus seemed to smile upon
Drake's cradle, his boyhood proved to be a very
stormy one indeed. He was not yet five when the
Protestant zeal of the Lord Protector Somerset
stirred the Roman Catholics of the West Country
into an insurrection that swept the anti-Papal
minority before it like flotsam before a flood.
Drake's father was a zealous Protestant, a 'hot
gospeller,' much given to preaching; and when he
was cast up by the storm on what is now Drake's
Island, just off Plymouth, he was glad to take
passage for Kent. His friends at court then
made him a sort of naval chaplain to the men who
took care of His Majesty's ships laid up in Gilling-
ham Reach on the River Medway, just below
where Chatham Dockyard stands to-day. Here,
in a vessel too old for service, most of Drake's
eleven brothers were born to a life as nearly
amphibious as the life of any boy could be. The
tide runs in with a rush from the sea at Sheerness,
only ten miles away; and so, among the creeks
and marshes, points and bends, through tortuous
channels and hurrying waters lashed by the keen

east wind of England, Drake reveled in the kind of
playground that a sea-dog's son should have.

During the reign of Mary (1553–58) 'hot gos-
pellers' like Drake's father were of course turned
out of the Service. And so young Francis had
to be apprenticed to 'the master of a bark, which
he used to coast along the shore, and sometimes
to carry merchandise into Zeeland and France.'
It was hard work and a rough life for the little
lad of ten. But Drake stuck to it, and 'so pleased
the old man by his industry that, being a bachelor,
at his death he bequeathed his bark unto him by
will and testament.' Moreover, after Elizabeth's
accession, Drake's father came into his own. He
took orders in the Church of England, and in
1561, when Francis was sixteen, became vicar
of Upchurch on the Medway, the same river on
which his boys had learned to live amphibious
lives.

No dreams of any Golden West had Drake
as yet. To the boy in his teens *Westward Ho!*
meant nothing more than the usual cry of London boatmen touting for fares up-stream. But,
before he went out with Sir John Hawkins, on
the 'troublesome' voyage which we have just
followed, he must have had a foretaste of some-

7

thing like his future raiding of the Spanish Main;
for the Channel swarmed with Protestant privateers, no gentler, when they caught a Spaniard,
than Spaniards were when they caught them.
He was twenty-two when he went out with Hawkins and would be in his twenty-fourth year when
he returned to England in the little *Judith* after
the murderous Spanish treachery at San Juan de
Ulua.

Just as the winter night was closing in, on the
20th of January, 1569, the *Judith* sailed into Plymouth. Drake landed. William Hawkins, John's
brother, wrote a petition to the Queen-in-Council
for letters-of-marque in reprisal for Ulua, and
Drake dashed off for London with the missive
almost before the ink was dry. Now it happened
that a Spanish treasure fleet, carrying money
from Italy and bound for Antwerp, had been
driven into Plymouth and neighboring ports by
Huguenot privateers. This money was urgently
needed by Alva, the very capable but ruthless
governor of the Spanish Netherlands, who, having
just drowned the rebellious Dutch in blood, was
now erecting a colossal statue to himself for
having ' extinguished sedition, chastised rebellion,

restored religion, secured justice, and established peace.' The Spanish ambassador therefore obtained leave to bring it overland to Dover.

But no sooner had Elizabeth signed the order of safe conduct than in came Drake with the news of San Juan de Ulua. Elizabeth at once saw that all the English sea-dogs would be flaming for revenge. Everyone saw that the treasure would be safer now in England than aboard any Spanish vessel in the Channel. So, on the ground that the gold, though payable to Philip's representative in Antwerp, was still the property of the Italian bankers who advanced it, Elizabeth sent orders down post-haste to commandeer it. The enraged ambassador advised Alva to seize everything English in the Netherlands. Elizabeth in turn seized everything Spanish in England. Elizabeth now held the diplomatic trumps; for existing treaties provided that there should be no reprisals without a reasonable delay; and Alva had seized English property before giving Elizabeth the customary time to explain.

John Hawkins entered Plymouth five days later than Drake and started for London with four pack horses carrying all he had saved from the wreck. By the irony of fate he travelled up

to town in the rear of the long procession that
carried the commandeered Spanish gold.

The plot thickened fast; for England was now
on the brink of war with France over the secret
aid Englishmen had been giving to the Huguenots
at La Rochelle. But suddenly Elizabeth was
all smiles and affability for France. And when
her two great merchant fleets put out to sea, one,
the wine-fleet, bound for La Rochelle, went with
only a small naval escort, just enough to keep
the pirates off; while the other, the big wool-
fleet, usually sent to Antwerp but now bound for
Hamburg, went with a strong fighting escort of
regular men-of-war.

Aboard this escort went Francis Drake as a
lieutenant in the Royal Navy. Home in June,
Drake ran down to Tavistock in Devon; wooed,
won, and married pretty Mary Newman, all
within a month. He was back on duty in July.

For the time being the war cloud passed away.
Elizabeth's tortuous diplomacy had succeeded,
owing to dissension among her enemies. In the
following year (1570) the international situation
was changed by the Pope, who issued a bull
formally deposing Elizabeth and absolving her
subjects from their allegiance to her. The French

and Spanish monarchs refused to publish this
order because they did not approve of deposition
by the Pope.   But, for all that, it worked against
Elizabeth by making her the official standing
enemy of Rome.   At the same time it worked
for her among the sea-dogs and all who thought
with them. 'The case,' said Thomas Fuller,
author of *The Worthies of England*, 'the case was
clear in *sea divinitie*.'   Religious zeal and commercial enterprise went hand in hand.   The case
was clear; and the English navy, now mobilized
and ready for war, made it much clearer still.

Westward Ho! in chief command, at the age of
twenty-five, with the tiny flotilla of the *Dragon*
and the *Swan*, manned by as good a lot of dare-
devil experts as any privateer could wish to see!
Out and back in 1570, and again in 1571, Drake
took reprisals on New Spain, made money for
all hands engaged, and gained a knowledge of
the American coast that stood him in good stead
for future expeditions.

It was 1572 when Drake, at the age of twenty-
seven, sailed out of Plymouth on the Nombre de
Dios expedition that brought him into fame.
He led a Lilliputian fleet: the *Pascha* and the

Swan, a hundred tons between them, with seventy-three men, all ranks and ratings, aboard of them. But both vessels were 'richly furnished with victuals and apparels for a whole year, and no less heedfully provided with all manner of ammunition, artillery [which then meant every kind of firearm as well as cannon], artificers' stuff and tools; but especially three dainty pinnaces made in Plymouth, taken asunder all in pieces,' and stowed aboard to be set up as occasion served.

Without once striking sail Drake made the channel between Dominica and Martinique in twenty-five days and arrived off a previously chosen secret harbor on the Spanish Main towards the end of July. To his intense surprise a column of smoke was rising from it, though there was no settlement within a hundred miles. On landing he found a leaden plate with this inscription: 'Captain Drake! If you fortune to come to this Port, make hast away! For the Spaniards which you had with you here, the last year, have bewrayed the place and taken away all that you left here. I depart hence, this present 7th of July, 1572. Your very loving friend, John Garrett.' That was fourteen days before. Drake, however, was determined to carry out his plan.

So he built a fort and set up his pinnaces. But others had now found the secret harbor; for in came three sail under Ranse, an Englishman, who asked that he be taken into partnership, which was done.

Then the combined forces, not much over a hundred strong, stole out and along the coast to the Isle of Pines, where again Drake found himself forestalled. From the negro crews of two Spanish vessels he discovered that, only six weeks earlier, the Maroons had annihilated a Spanish force on the Isthmus and nearly taken Nombre de Dios itself. These Maroons were the descendants of escaped negro slaves intermarried with the most warlike of the Indians. They were regular desperadoes, always, and naturally, at war with the Spaniards, who treated them as vermin to be killed at sight. Drake put the captured negroes ashore to join the Maroons, with whom he always made friends. Then with seventy-three picked men he made his dash for Nombre de Dios, leaving the rest under Ranse to guard the base.

Nombre de Dios was the Atlantic terminus, as Panama was the Pacific terminus, of the treasure trail across the Isthmus of Darien. The Spaniards, knowing nothing of Cape Horn, and unable to face the appalling dangers of Magellan's straits, used to bring the Peruvian treasure ships to Panama, whence the treasure was taken across the isthmus to Nombre de Dios by *recuas*, that is, by mule trains under escort.

At evening Drake's vessel stood off the harbor of Nombre de Dios and stealthily approached unseen. It was planned to make the landing in the morning. A long and nerve-racking wait ensued. As the hours dragged on, Drake felt instinctively that his younger men were getting demoralized. They began to whisper about the size of the town — 'as big as Plymouth' — with perhaps a whole battalion of the famous Spanish infantry, and so on. It wanted an hour of the first real streak of dawn. But just then the old moon sent a ray of light quivering in on the tide. Drake instantly announced the dawn, issued the orders: 'Shove off, out oars, give way!' Inside the bay a ship just arrived from sea was picking up her moorings. A boat left her side and pulled like mad for the wharf. But Drake's men raced the Spaniards, beat them, and made them sheer off to a landing some way beyond the town.

Springing   eagerly   ashore   the   Englishmen

tumbled the Spanish guns off their platforms while the astonished sentry ran for dear life. In five minutes the church bells were pealing out their wild alarms, trumpet calls were sounding, drums were beating round the general parade, and the civilians of the place, expecting massacre at the hands of the Maroons, were rushing about in agonized confusion. Drake's men fell in — they were all well-drilled — and were quickly told off into three detachments. The largest under Drake, the next under Oxenham — the hero of Kingsley's *Westward Ho!* — and the third, of twelve men only, to guard the pinnaces. Having found that the new fort on the hill commanding the town was not yet occupied, Drake and Oxenham marched against the town at the head of their sixty men, Oxenham by a flank, Drake straight up the main street, each with a trumpet sounding, a drum rolling, fire-pikes blazing, swords flashing, and all ranks yelling like fiends. Drake was only of medium stature. But he had the strength of a giant, the pluck of a bulldog, the spring of a tiger, and the cut of a man that is born to command. Broad-browed, with steel-blue eyes and close-cropped auburn hair and beard, he was all kindliness of countenance to friends, but a very 'Dragon' to his Spanish foes.

As Drake's men reached the Plaza, his trumpeter blew one blast of defiance and then fell dead. Drake returned the Spanish volley and charged immediately, the drummer beating furiously, pikes levelled, and swords brandished. The Spaniards did not wait for him to close; for Oxenham's party, fire-pikes blazing, were taking them in flank. ‾ Out went the Spaniards through the Panama gate, with screaming townsfolk scurrying before them. Bang went the gate, now under English guard, as Drake made for the Governor's house. There lay a pile of silver bars such as his men had never dreamt of: in all, about four hundred tons of silver ready for the homeward fleet — enough not only to fill but sink the *Pascha*, *Swan*, and pinnaces. But silver was then no more to Drake than it was once to Solomon. What he wanted were the diamonds and pearls and gold, which were stored, he learned, in the King's Treasure House beside the bay.

A terrific storm now burst. The fire-pikes and arquebuses had to be taken under cover. The wall of the King's Treasure House defied all efforts to breach it. And the Spaniards who had been shut into the town, discovering how few the English were, reformed for attack. Some of Drake's men began to lose heart. But in a moment he stepped to the front and ordered Oxenham to go round and smash in the Treasure House gate while he held the Plaza himself. Just as the men stepped off, however, he reeled aside and fell. He had fainted from loss of blood caused by a wound he had managed to conceal. There was no holding the men now. They gave him a cordial, after which he bound up his leg, for he was a first-rate surgeon, and repeated his orders as before. But there were a good many wounded; and, with Drake no longer able to lead, the rest all begged to go back. So back to their boats they went, and over to the Bastimentos or Victualling Islands, which contained the gardens and poultry runs of the Nombre de Dios citizens.

Here they were visited, under a flag of truce, by the Spanish officer commanding the reinforcement just sent across from Panama. He was all politeness, airs, and graces, while trying to ferret out the secret of their real strength. Drake, however, was not to be outdone either in diplomacy or war; and a delightful little comedy of

prying and veiling courtesies was played out,
to the great amusement of the English sea-dogs.
Finally, when the time agreed upon was up, the
Spanish officer departed, pouring forth a stream of
high-flown compliments, which Drake, who was a
Spanish scholar, answered with the like. Waving
each other a ceremonious adieu the two leaders
were left no wiser than before.

Nombre de Dios, now strongly reinforced and
on its guard, was not an easy nut to crack. But
Panama? Panama meant a risky march inland
and a still riskier return by the regular treasure
trail. But with the help of the Maroons, who
knew the furtive byways to a foot, the thing
might yet be done. Ranse thought the game not
worth the candle and retired from the partnership,
much to Drake's delight.

A good preliminary stroke was made by raiding Cartagena. Here Drake found a frigate deserted by its crew, who had gone ashore to see
fair play in a duel fought about a seaman's mistress. The old man left in charge confessed that
a Seville ship was round the point. Drake cut
her out at once, in spite of being fired at from the
shore. Next, in came two more Spanish sail to
warn Cartagena that 'Captain Drake has been

at Nombre de Dios and taken it, and if a blest
bullet hadn't hit him in the leg he would have
sacked it too.'

Cartagena, however, was up in arms already;
so Drake put all his prisoners ashore unhurt and
retired to reconsider his position, leaving Diego,
a negro fugitive from Nombre de Dios, to muster
the Maroons for a raid overland to Panama.
Then Drake, who sank the *Swan* and burnt his
prizes because he had only men enough for the
Pascha and the pinnaces, disappeared into a new
secret harbor. But his troubles were only beginning; for word came that the Maroons said
that nothing could be done inland till the rains
were over, five months hence. This meant a
long wait; however, what with making supply
depots and picking up prizes here and there, the
wet time might pass off well enough.

One day Oxenham's crew nearly mutinied over
the shortness of provisions. 'Have ye not as
much as I,' Drake called to them, 'and has God's
Providence ever failed us yet?' Within an hour
a Spanish vessel hove in sight, making such very
heavy weather of it that boarding her was out of
the question. But 'We spent not two hours in
attendance till it pleased God to send us a reason-

able calm, so that we might use our guns and approach her at pleasure. We found her laden with victuals, which we received as sent of God's great mercy.' Then 'Yellow Jack' broke out, and the men began to fall sick and die. The company consisted of seventy-three men; and twenty-eight of these perished of the fever, among them the surgeon himself and Drake's own brother.

But on the 3d of February, 1573, Drake was ready for the dash on Panama. Leaving behind about twenty-five men to guard the base, he began the overland march with a company of fifty, all told, of whom thirty-one were picked Maroons. The fourth day out Drake climbed a forest giant on the top of the Divide, saw the Atlantic behind him and the Pacific far in front, and vowed that if he lived he would sail an English ship over the great South Sea. Two days more and the party left the protecting forest for the rolling pampas where the risk of being seen increased at every step. Another day's march and Panama was sighted as they topped the crest of one of the bigger waves of ground. A clever Maroon went ahead to spy out the situation and returned to say that two *recuas* would leave at dusk, one

coming from Venta Cruz, fifteen miles northwest
of Panama, carrying silver and supplies, and the
other from Panama, loaded with jewels and gold.
Then a Spanish sentry was caught asleep by the
advanced party of Maroons, who smelt him out
by the match of his fire-lock. In his gratitude
for being protected from the Maroons, this man
confirmed the previous information.

The excitement now was most intense; for the
crowning triumph of a two-years' great adventure was at last within striking distance of the
English crew. Drake drew them up in proper
order; and every man took off his shirt and put
it on again outside his coat, so that each would
recognize the others in the night attack. Then
they lay listening for the mule-bells, till presently
the warning tinkle let them know that *recuas*
were approaching from both Venta Cruz and
Panama. The first, or silver train from Venta
Cruz, was to pass in silence; only the second,
or gold train from Panama, was to be attacked.
Unluckily one of the Englishmen had been secretly
taking pulls at his flask and had just become pot-
valiant when a stray Spanish gentleman came
riding up from Venta Cruz. The Englishman
sprang to his feet, swayed about, was tripped up

by Maroons and promptly sat upon. But the
Spaniard saw his shirt, reined up, whipped round,
and galloped back to Panama. This took place
so silently at the extreme flank in towards Panama
that it was not observed by Drake or any other
Englishman. Presently what appeared to be
the gold train came within range. Drake blew
his whistle; and all set on with glee, only to find
that the Panama *recua* they were attacking was
a decoy sent on to spring the trap and that the
gold and jewels had been stopped.

The Spaniards were up in arms. But Drake
slipped away through the engulfing forest and
came out on the Atlantic side, where he found his
rear-guard intact and eager for further exploits.
He was met by Captain Têtu, a Huguenot just
out from France, with seventy men. Têtu gave
Drake news of the Massacre of St. Bartholomew,
and this drew the French and English Protestants
together. They agreed to engage in further
raiding of Spaniards, share and share alike by
nationalities, though Drake had now only thirty-
one men against Têtu's seventy. Nombre de
Dios, they decided, was not vulnerable, as all
the available Spanish forces were concentrated
there for its defence, and so they planned to seize

a Spanish train of gold and jewels just far enough inland to give them time to get away with the plunder before the garrison could reach them. Somewhere on the coast they established a base of operations and then marched overland to the Panama trail and lay in wait.

This time the marauders were successful. When the Spanish train of gold and jewels came opposite the ambush, Drake's whistle blew. The leading mules were stopped. The rest lay down, as mule-trains will. The guard was overpowered after killing a Maroon and wounding Captain Têtu. And when the garrison of Nombre de Dios arrived a few hours later the gold and jewels had all gone.

For a day and a night and another day Drake and his men pushed on, loaded with plunder, back to their rendezvous along the coast, leaving Têtu and two of his devoted Frenchmen to be rescued later. When they arrived, worn out, at the rendezvous, not a man was in sight. Drake built a raft out of unhewn tree trunks and, setting up a biscuit bag as a sail, pushed out with two Frenchmen and one Englishman till he found his boats. The plunder was then divided up between the French and the English, while Oxenham headed

8

a rescue party to bring Têtu to the coast. One Frenchman was found. But Têtu and the other had been caught by Spaniards.

The *Pascha* was given to the accumulated Spanish prisoners to sail away in. The pinnaces were kept till a suitable, smart-sailing Spanish craft was found, boarded, and captured to replace them; whereupon they were broken up and their metal given to the Maroons. Then, in two frigates, with ballast of silver and cargo of jewels and gold, the thirty survivors of the adventure set sail for home. 'Within 23 days we passed from the Cape of Florida to the Isles of Scilly, and so arrived at Plymouth on Sunday about sermon time, August 9, 1573, at what time the news of our Captain's return, brought unto his friends, did so speedily pass over all the church, and surpass their minds with desire to see him, that very few or none remained with the preacher, all hastening to see the evidence of God's love and blessing towards our Gracious Queen and country, by the fruit of our Captain's labour and success. *Soli Deo Gloria.*'

CHAPTER VII

DRAKE'S 'ENCOMPASSMENT OF ALL THE WORLDE'

WHEN Drake left for Nombre de Dios in the spring of 1572, Spain and England were both ready to fly at each other's throats. When he came back in the summer of 1573, they were all for making friends — hypocritically so, but friends. Drake's plunder stank in the nostrils of the haughty Dons. It was a very inconvenient factor in the diplomatic problem for Elizabeth. Therefore Drake disappeared and his plunder too. He went to Ireland on service in the navy. His plunder was divided up in secrecy among all the high and low contracting parties.

In 1574 the Anglo-Spanish scene had changed again. The Spaniards had been so harassed by the English sea-dogs between the Netherlands and Spain that Philip listened to his great admiral, Menendez, who, despairing of direct attack on England, proposed to seize the Scilly Isles and

from that naval base clear out a way through all
the pirates of the English Channel.   War seemed
certain.   But a terrible epidemic broke out in
the Spanish fleet. Menendez died. And Philip
changed his policy again.

This same year John Oxenham, Drake's old
second-in-command, sailed over to his death.
The Spaniards caught him on the Isthmus of
Darien and hanged him as a pirate at Lima in
Peru.

In the autumn of 1575 Drake returned to England with a new friend, Thomas Doughty, a
soldier-scholar of the Renaissance, clever and
good company, but one of those 'Italianate' Englishmen who gave rise to the Italian proverb:
Inglese italianato è diavolo incarnato — 'an Italian-
ized Englishman is the very Devil.' Doughty
was patronized by the Earl of Essex, who had
great influence at court.

The next year, 1576, is noted for the 'Spanish
Fury.' Philip's sea power was so hampered by the
Dutch and English privateers, and he was so im-
potent against the English navy, that he could get
no ready money, either by loan or from America,
to pay his troops in Antwerp. These men, reinforced by others, therefore mutinied and sacked

the whole of Antwerp, killing all who opposed them and practically ruining the city from which Charles V used to draw such splendid subsidies. The result was a strengthening of Dutch resistance everywhere.

Elizabeth had been unusually tortuous in her policy about this time. But in 1577 she was ready for another shot at Spain, provided always that it entailed no open war. Don John of Austria, natural son of Charles V, had all the shining qualities that his legitimate half-brother Philip lacked. He was the hero of Lepanto and had offered to conquer the Moors in Tunis if Philip would let him rule as king. Philip, crafty, cold, and jealous, of course refused and sent him to the Netherlands instead. Here Don John formed the still more aspiring plan of pacifying the Dutch, marrying Mary Queen of Scots, deposing Elizabeth, and reigning over all the British Isles. The Pope had blessed both schemes. But the Dutch insisted on the immediate withdrawal of the Spanish troops. This demolished Don John's plan. But it pleased Philip, who could now ruin his brilliant brother by letting him wear himself out by trying to govern the Netherlands without an army. Then the Duke of Anjou, brother to the King of France, came into the fast-thickening plot at the head of the French rescuers of the Netherlands from Spain. But a victorious French army in the Netherlands was worse for England than even Spanish rule there. So Elizabeth tried to support the Dutch enough to annoy Philip and at the same time keep them independent of the French.

In her desire to support them against Philip indirectly she found it convenient to call Drake into consultation. Drake then presented to Sir Francis Walsingham his letter of commendation from the Earl of Essex, under whom he had served in Ireland; whereupon 'Secretary Walsingham [the first civilian who ever grasped the principle of modern sea power] declared that Her Majesty had received divers injuries of the King of Spain, for which she desired revenge. He showed me a plot [map] willing me to note down where he might be most annoyed. But I refused to set my hand to anything, affirming that Her Majesty was mortal, and that if it should please God to take Her Majesty away that some prince might reign that might be in league with the King of Spain, and then would my own hand be a witness against myself.' Elizabeth was forty-four. Mary

Queen of Scots was watching for the throne. Plots and counter-plots were everywhere.

Shortly after this interview Drake was told late at night that he should have audience of Her Majesty next day. On seeing him, Elizabeth went straight to the point. 'Drake, I would gladly be revenged on the King of Spain for divers injuries that I have received.' 'And withal,' says Drake, 'craved my advice therein; who told Her Majesty the only way was to annoy him by the Indies.' On that he disclosed his whole daring scheme for raiding the Pacific. Elizabeth, who, like her father, 'loved a man' who was a man, fell in with this at once. Secrecy was of course essential. 'Her Majesty did swear by her Crown that if any within her realm did give the King of Spain to understand hereof they should lose their heads therefor.' At a subsequent audience 'Her Majesty gave me special commandment that of all men my Lord Treasurer should not know of it.' The cautious Lord Treasurer Burleigh was against what he considered dangerous forms of privateering and was for keeping on good terms with Spanish arms and trade as long as possible. Mendoza, lynx-eyed ambassador of Spain, was hoodwinked. But

Doughty, the viper in Drake's bosom, was medi-
tating mischief: not exactly treason with Spain,
but at least a breach of confidence by telling
Burleigh.

De Guaras, chief Spanish spy in England, was
sorely puzzled. Drake's ostensible destination
was Egypt, and his men were openly enlisted for
Alexandria. The Spaniards, however, saw far
enough through this to suppose that he was really
going back to Nombre de Dios. It did not seem
likely, though quite possible, that he was going
in search of the Northwest Passage, for Martin
Frobisher had gone out on that quest the year
before and had returned with a lump of black
stone from the arctic desolation of Baffin Island.
No one seems to have divined the truth. Cape
Horn was unknown. The Strait of Magellan
was supposed to be the only opening between
South America and a huge antarctic continent,
and its reputation for disasters had grown so terrible, and rightly terrible, that it had been given
up as the way into the Pacific. The Spanish way,
as we have seen, was overland from Nombre de
Dios to Panama, more or less along the line of
the modern Panama Canal.

In the end Drake got away quietly enough,

on the 15th of November, 1577. The court and country were in great excitement over the conspiracy between the Spaniards and Mary Queen of Scots, now a prisoner of nine years' standing.

'THE FAMOUS VOYAGE OF SIR FRANCIS DRAKE *into the South Sea, and therehence about the whole Globe of the Earth, begun in the year of our Lord 1577*' well deserves its great renown. Drake's flotilla seems absurdly small. But, for its own time, it was far from insignificant; and it was exceedingly well found. The *Pelican*, afterwards called the *Golden Hind*, though his flagship, was of only a hundred tons. The *Elizabeth*, the *Swan*, the *Marigold*, and the *Benedict* were of eighty, fifty, thirty, and fifteen. There were altogether less than three hundred tons and two hundred men. The crews numbered a hundred and fifty. The rest were gentlemen-adventurers, special artificers, two trained surveyors, musicians, boys, and Drake's own page, Jack Drake. There was 'great store of wild-fire, chain-shot, harquebusses, pistols, corslets, bows and other like weapons in great abundance. Neither had he omitted to make provision for ornament and delight, carrying with him expert musicians, rich furniture (all the vessels for his table, yea, many belonging even to the cook-room, being of pure silver), and divers shows of all sorts of curious workmanship whereby the civility and magnificence of his native country might amongst all nations withersoever he should come, be the more admired.'[1]

[1] The little handbook issued by Pette and Jackman in 1580, for those whom we should now call commercial travellers, is full of 'tips' about ' Thinges to be carried with you, whereof more or lesse is to be carried for a shewe of our commodities to bee made.' For instance:—'Kersies of all orient coulours, specially of stamel [fine worsted], brode cloth of orient coulours also. Taffeta hats. Deepe cappes for mariners. Quilted Cappes of Levant Taffeta of divers coulours, for the night. Garters of Silke. Girdels of Buffe and all leathers, with gilt and ungilt Buckles, specially wast girdels. Wast girdels of velvet. Gloves of all sortes, knit and of leather. Gloves perfumed. Shooes of Spanish leather, of divers colours. Looking glasses for Women, great and fayre. Comes of Ivorie. Handkerchewes, with silk of divers colours, wrought. Glasen eyes to ride with against dust [so motor goggles are not so new, after all!]. Boxes with weightes of golde, and every kind of coyne of golde, to shewe that the people here use weight and measure, which is a certayne showe of wisedome, and of a certayne government settled here.'

There are also elaborate directions about what to take 'For banketing on shipborde of persons of credite' [and prospective customers]. 'First, the sweetest perfumes to set under hatches to make the place smell sweete against their coming aborde. Marmelade. Sucket [candies]. Figges barrelled. Raisins of the Sun. Comfets that shall not dissolve. Prunes damaske. Dried peres. Walnuttes. Almondes. Olives, to make them taste their wine. The Apple John that dureth two yeares, to make showe of our fruites. Hullocke [a sweet wine]. Sacke. Vials of good sweet waters, and casting-bottels of glass, to besprinckel the gests withal, after their coming aborde. The sweet oyle of Zante and excellent French vinegar and a fine kind of Bisket steeped in the same do make a banketting dishe,

Sou'sou'west went Drake's flotilla and made its landfall 'towards the Pole Antartick' off the 'Land of Devils' in 31° 40' south, northeast of Montevideo. Frightful storms had buffeted the little ships about for weary weeks together, and all hands thought they were the victims of some magician on board, perhaps the 'Italianate' Doughty, or else of native witchcraft from the shore. The experienced old pilot, who was a Portuguese, explained that the natives had sold themselves to Devils, who were kinder masters than the Spaniards, and that 'now when they see ships they cast sand into the air, whereof ariseth a most gross thick fogg and palpable

---

and a little Sugar cast in it cooleth and comforteth, and refresheth the spirittes of man. Synomomme Water and Imperiall Water is to be had with you to comfort your sicke in the voyage.'

No feature is neglected. 'Take with you the large mappe of London and let the river be drawn full of shippes to make the more showe of your great trade. The booke of the Attyre of All Nations carried with you and bestowed in gift would be much esteemed. Tinder boxes, with steel, flint, and matches. A painted Bellowes, for perhaps they have not the use of them. All manner of edge tools. Note specially what dyeing they use.' After many more items the authors end up with two bits of good advice. 'Take with you those things that bee in the Perfection of Goodnesse to make your commodities in credit in time to come.' 'Learn what the Country hath before you offer your commodities for sale; for if you bring thither what you yourself desire to lade yourself home with, you must not sell yours deare lest hereafter you purchase theirs not so cheape as you would.'

darkness, and withal horrible, fearful, and intolerable winds, rains, and storms.'

But witchcraft was not Thomas Doughty's real offence. Even before leaving England, and after betraying Elizabeth and Drake to Burleigh, who wished to curry favor with the Spanish traders rather than provoke the Spanish power, Doughty was busy tampering with the men. A storekeeper had to be sent back for peculation designed to curtail Drake's range of action. Then Doughty tempted officers and men: talked up the terrors of Magellan's Strait, ran down his friend's authority, and finally tried to encourage downright desertion by underhand means. This was too much for Drake. Doughty was arrested, tied to the mast, and threatened with dire punishment if he did not mend his ways. But he would not mend his ways. He had a brother on board and a friend, a 'very craftie lawyer'; so stern measures were soon required. Drake held a sort of court-martial which condemned Doughty to death. Then Doughty, having played his last card and lost, determined to die 'like an officer and gentleman.'

Drake solemnly 'pronounced him the child of Death and persuaded him that he would by these

means make him the servant of God.' Doughty
fell in with the idea and the former friends took the
Sacrament together, 'for which Master Doughty
gave him hearty thanks, never otherwise terming
him than "My good Captaine."' Chaplain
Fletcher having ended with the absolution, Drake
and Doughty sat down together 'as cheerfully
as ever in their lives, each cheering up the other
and taking their leave by drinking to each other,
as if some journey had been in hand.' Then
Drake and Doughty went aside for a private
conversation of which no record has remained.
After this Doughty walked to the place of execution, where, like King Charles I,

> He nothing common did or mean
> Upon that memorable scene.

'And so bidding the whole company farewell he
laid his head on the block.' 'Lo! this is the end
of traitors!' said Drake as the executioner raised
the head aloft.

Drake, like Magellan, decided to winter where
he was, in Port St. Julian on the east coast of
Patagonia. His troubles with the men were not
yet over; for the soldiers resented being put on

an equality with the sailors, and the 'very craftie lawyer' and Doughty's brother were anything but pleased with the turn events had taken. Then, again, the faint-hearts murmured in their storm-beaten tents against the horrors of the awful Straits. So Drake resolved to make things clear for good and all. Unfolding a document he began: 'My Masters, I am a very bad orator, for my bringing up hath not been in learning, but what I shall speak here let every man take good notice of and let him write it down; for I will speak nothing but I will answer it in England, yea, and before Her Majesty, and I have it here already set down.' Then, after reminding them of the great adventure before them and saying that mutiny and dissension must stop at once, he went on: 'For by the life of God it doth even take my wits from me to think of it. Here is such controversy between the gentlemen and sailors that it doth make me mad to hear it. I must have the gentleman to haul with the mariner and the mariner with the gentleman. I would know him that would refuse to set his hand to a rope! But I know there is not any such here.' To those whose hearts failed them he offered the *Marigold*. 'But let them go homeward;

for if I find them in my way, I will surely sink them.' Not a man stepped forward. Then, turning to the officers, he discharged every one of them for re-appointment at his pleasure. Next, he made the worst offenders, the 'craftie lawyer' included, step to the front for reprimand. Finally, producing the Queen's commission, he ended by a ringing appeal to their united patriotism. 'We have set by the ears three mighty Princes [the sovereigns of England, Spain, and Portugal]; and if this voyage should not have success we should not only be a scorning unto our enemies but a blot on our country for ever. What triumph would it not be for Spain and Portugal! The like of this would never more be tried.' Then he gave back every man his rank again, explaining that he and they were all servants of Her Majesty together. With this the men marched off, loyal and obedient, to their tents.

Next week Drake sailed for the much dreaded Straits, before entering which he changed the *Pelican's* name to the *Golden Hind*, which was the crest of Sir Christopher Hatton, one of the chief promoters of the enterprise and also one of Doughty's patrons. Then every vessel struck her topsail to the bunt in honor of the Queen as well as to show that all discoveries and captures were to be made in her sole name. Seventeen days of appalling dangers saw them through the Straits, where icy squalls came rushing down from every quarter of the baffling channels. But the Pacific was still worse. For no less than fifty-two consecutive days a furious gale kept driving them about like so many bits of driftwood. 'The like of it no traveller hath felt, neither hath there ever been such a tempest since Noah's flood.' The little English vessels fought for their very lives in that devouring hell of waters, the loneliest and most stupendous in the world. The *Marigold* went down with all hands, and Parson Fletcher, who heard their dying call, thought it was a judgment. At last the gale abated near Cape Horn, where Drake landed with a compass, while Parson Fletcher set up a stone engraved with the Queen's name and the date of the discovery.

Deceived by the false trend of the coast shown on the Spanish charts Drake went a long way northwest from Cape Horn. Then he struck in northeast and picked up the Chilean Islands. It was December, 1578; but not a word of warning had reached the Spanish Pacific when Drake stood in to Valparaiso. Seeing a sail, the crew of the *Grand Captain of the South* got up a cask of wine and beat a welcome on their drums. In the twinkling of an eye gigantic Tom Moone was over the side at the head of a party of boarders who laid about them with a will and soon drove the Spaniards below. Half a million dollars' worth of gold and jewels was taken with this prize.

Drake then found a place in Salado Bay where he could clean the *Golden Hind* while the pinnace ranged south to look for the other ships that had parted company during the two months' storm. These were never found, the *Elizabeth* and the *Swan* having gone home after parting company in the storm that sank the *Marigold*. After a prolonged search the *Golden Hind* stood north again. Meanwhile the astounding news of her arrival was spreading dismay all over the coast, where the old Spanish governor's plans were totally upset. The Indians had just been defeated when this strange ship came sailing in from nowhere, to the utter confusion of their enemies. The governor died of vexation, and all the Spanish authorities were nearly worried to death. They had never dreamt of such an invasion. Their crews were small, their lumbering

9

vessels very lightly armed, their towns unforti-
fied.

But Drake went faster by sea than their news
by land. Every vessel was overhauled, taken,
searched, emptied of its treasure, and then sent
back with its crew and passengers at liberty.
One day a watering party chanced upon a Spaniard from Potosi fast asleep with thirteen bars
of silver by him. The bars were lifted quietly
and the Spaniard left sleeping peacefully. Another Spaniard suddenly came round a corner
with half a ton of silver on eight llamas. The
Indians came off to trade; and Drake, as usual,
made friends with them at once. He had already
been attacked by other Indians on both coasts.
But this was because the unknown English had
been mistaken for the hated Spaniards.

As he neared Lima, Drake quickened his pace
lest the great annual treasure ship of 1579 should
get wind of what was wrong. A minor treasure
ship was found to have been cleared of all her
silver just in time to balk him. So he set every
stitch of canvas she possessed and left her driving
out to sea with two other empty prizes. Then
he stole into Lima after dark and came to anchor
surrounded by Spanish vessels not one of which

had set a watch. They were found nearly empty. But a ship from Panama looked promising; so the pinnace started after her, but was fired on and an Englishman was killed. Drake then followed her, after cutting every cable in the harbor, which soon became a pandemonium of vessels gone adrift. The Panama ship had nothing of great value except her news, which was that the great treasure ship *Nuestra Señora de la Concepcion*, 'the chiefest glory of the whole South Sea,' was on her way to Panama.

She had a very long start; and, as ill luck would have it, Drake got becalmed outside Callao, where the bells rang out in wild alarm. The news had spread inland and the Viceroy of Peru came hurrying down with all the troops that he could muster. Finding from some arrows that the strangers were Englishmen, he put four hundred soldiers into the only two vessels that had escaped the general wreck produced by Drake's cutting of the cables. When Drake saw the two pursuing craft, he took back his prize crew from the Panama vessel, into which he put his prisoners. Meanwhile a breeze sprang up and he soon drew far ahead. The Spanish soldiers overhauled the Panama prize and gladly gave up the pursuit.

They had no guns of any size with which to fight the *Golden Hind;* and most of them were so sea-sick from the heaving ground-swell that they couldn't have boarded her in any case.

Three more prizes were then taken by the swift *Golden Hind.* Each one had news which showed that Drake was closing on the chase. Another week passed with every stitch of canvas set. A fourth prize, taken off Cape San Francisco, said that the treasure ship was only one day ahead. But she was getting near to Panama; so every nerve was strained anew. Presently Jack Drake, the Captain's page, yelled out *Sail-ho!* and scrambled down the mainmast to get the golden chain that Drake had promised to the first lookout who saw the chase. It was ticklish work, so near to Panama; and local winds might ruin all. So Drake, in order not to frighten her, trailed a dozen big empty wine jars over the stern to moderate his pace. At eight o'clock the jars were cut adrift and the *Golden Hind* sprang forward with the evening breeze, her crew at battle quarters and her decks all cleared for action. The chase was called the 'Spitfire' by the Spaniards because she was much better armed than any other vessel there. But, all the same, her armament was nothing for her tonnage. The Spaniards trusted to their remoteness for protection; and that was their undoing.

To every Englishman's amazement the chase was seen to go about and calmly come to hail the *Golden Hind*, which she mistook for a despatch vessel sent after her with some message from the Viceroy! Drake, asking nothing better, ran up alongside as Anton her captain hailed him with a *Who are you? A ship of Chili!* answered Drake. Anton looked down on the stranger's deck to see it full of armed men from whom a roar of triumph came. *English! strike sail!* Then Drake's whistle blew sharply and instant silence followed; on which he hailed Don Anton: — *Strike sail! Señor Juan de Anton, or I must send you to the bottom!* —*Come aboard and do it yourself!* bravely answered Anton. Drake's whistle blew one shrill long blast, which loosed a withering volley at less than point-blank range. Anton tried to bear away and shake off his assailant. But in vain. The English guns now opened on his masts and rigging. Down came the mizzen, while a hail of English shot and arrows prevented every attempt to clear away the wreckage. The dumbfounded Spanish crew ran below. Don Anton looked

overside to port; and there was the English
pinnace, from which forty English boarders were
nimbly climbing up his own ship's side. Resistance was hopeless; so Anton struck and was
taken aboard the *Golden Hind*. There he met
Drake, who was already taking off his armor.
'Accept with patience the usage of war,' said
Drake, laying his hand on Anton's shoulder.

For all that night, next day, and the next night
following Drake sailed west with his fabulous prize
so as to get well clear of the trade route along the
coast. What the whole treasure was has never
been revealed. But it certainly amounted to
the equivalent of many millions at the present
day. Among the official items were: 13 chests
of pieces of eight, 80 lbs. of pure gold, jewels and
plate, 26 ton weight of silver, and sundries
unspecified. As the Spanish pilot's son looked over
the rail at this astounding sight, the Englishmen
called out to say that his father was no longer the
pilot of the old Spit-*fire* but of the new Spit-*silver*.

The prisoners were no less gratified than surprised by Drake's kind treatment. He enter-
tained Don Anton at a banquet, took him all over
the *Golden Hind*, and entrusted him with a message to Don Martin, the traitor of San Juan de

Ulua. This was to say that if Don Martin hanged any more Englishmen, as he had just hanged Oxenham, he should soon be given a present of two thousand Spanish heads. Then Drake gave every Spanish officer and man a personal gift proportioned to his rank, put all his accumulated prisoners aboard the emptied treasure ship, wished them a prosperous voyage and better luck next time, furnished the brave Don Anton with a letter of protection in case he should fall in with an English vessel, and, after many expressions of goodwill on both sides, sailed north, the voyage 'made'; while the poor 'spit-silver' treasure ship turned sadly east and steered for Panama.

Lima, Panama, and Nombre de Dios were in wild commotion at the news; and every sailor and soldier that the Spaniards had was going to and fro, uncertain whether to attack or to defend, and still more distracted as to the most elusive English whereabouts. One good Spanish captain, Don Pedro Sarmiento de Gamboa, was all for going north, his instinct telling him that Drake would not come back among the angry bees after stealing all the honey. But, by the time the Captain-General of New Spain had made up his mind to take one of the many wrong directions he had been thinking of, Drake was already far on his way north to found New Albion.

Drake's triumph over all difficulties had won the hearts of his men more than ever before, while the capture of the treasure ship had done nothing to loosen the bonds of discipline. Don Francisco de Zarate wrote a very intimate account of his experience as a prisoner on board the *Golden Hind.* 'The English captain is one of the greatest mariners at sea, alike from his skill and his powers of command. His ship is a very fast sailer and her men are all skilled hands of warlike age and so well trained that they might be old soldiers of the Italian tertias,' the crack corps of the age in Spanish eyes. 'He is served with much plate and has all possible kinds of delicacies and scents, many of which he says the Queen of England gave him. None of the gentlemen sit or cover in his presence without first being ordered to do so. They dine and sup to the music of violins. His galleon carries about thirty guns and a great deal of ammunition.' This was in marked contrast to the common Spanish practice, even on the Atlantic side. The greedy exploiters of New Spain grudged every ton of armament

and every well-trained fighting sailor, both on
account of the expense and because this form of
protection took up room they wished to fill with
merchandise. The result was, of course, that they
lost more by capture than they gained by evad-
ing the regulation about the proper armament.
'His ship is not only of the very latest type but
sheathed.' Before copper sheathing was invented
some generations later, the Teredo worm used to
honeycomb unprotected hulls in the most dangerous way. John Hawkins invented the sheathing
used by Drake: a good thick tar-and-hair sheeting
clamped on with elm.

Northwest to Coronado, then to Aguatulco,
then fifteen hundred miles due west, brought
Drake about that distance west-by-south of the
modern San Francisco. Here he turned east-
north-east and, giving the land a wide berth,
went on to perhaps the latitude of Vancouver
Island, always looking for the reverse way through
America by the fabled Northwest Passage. Either
there was the most extraordinary June ever
known in California and Oregon, or else the nar-
ratives of those on board have all been hopelessly
confused, for freezing rain is said to have fallen
on the night of June the 3d in the latitude of 42°.

In 48° 'there followed most vile, thick, and
stinking fogs' with still more numbing cold. The
meat froze when taken off the fire. The wet
rigging turned to icicles. Six men could hardly
do the work of three. Fresh from the tropics,
the crews were unfit for going any farther. A
tremendous nor'wester settled the question, any-
way; and Drake ran south to 38° 30', where,
in what is now Drake's Bay, he came to anchor
just north of San Francisco.

Not more than once, if ever at all, and that a
generation earlier, had Europeans been in northern
California. The Indians took the Englishmen
for gods whom they knew not whether to love or
fear. Drake with the essential kindliness of most,
and the magnetic power of all, great born commanders, soon won the natives' confidence. But
their admiration 'as men ravished in their minds'
was rather overpowering; for, after 'a kind of
most lamentable weeping and crying out,' they
came forward with various offerings for the new-
found gods, prostrating themselves in humble
adoration and tearing their breasts and faces in a
wild desire to show the spirit of self-sacrifice.
Drake and his men, all Protestants, were horrified
at being made what they considered idols. So,

kneeling down, they prayed aloud, raising hands
and eyes to Heaven, hoping thereby to show the
heathen where the true God lived. Drake then
read the Bible and all the Englishmen sang
Psalms, the Indians, 'observing the end of every
pause, with one voice still cried *Oh!* greatly re-
joicing in our exercises.' As this impromptu
service ended the Indians gave back all the presents Drake had given them and retired in attitudes
of adoration.

In three days more they returned, headed
by a Medicine-man, whom the English called
the 'mace-bearer.' With the slow and stately
measure of a mystic dance this great high priest
of heathen rites advanced chanting a sort of litany.
Both litany and dance were gradually taken up
by tens, by hundreds, and finally by all the
thousands of the devotees, who addressed Drake
with shouts of *Hyoh!* and invested him with a
headdress of rare plumage and a necklace of quaint
beads. It was, in fact, a native coronation without a soul to doubt the divine right of their new
king. Drake's Protestant scruples were quieted
by thinking 'to what good end God had brought
this to pass, and what honour and profit it might
bring to our country in time to come. So, in

the name and to the use of her most excellent
Majesty, he took the sceptre, crown, and dignity'
and proclaimed an English protectorate over the
land he called New Albion. He then set up a
brass plate commemorating this proclamation,
and put an English coin in the middle so that the
Indians might see Elizabeth's portrait and armorial
device.

The exaltation of the ecstatic devotees continued till the day he left. They crowded in to be
cured by the touch of his hand — those were the
times in which the sovereign was expected to
cure the King's Evil by a touch. They also
expected to be cured by inhaling the divine breath
of any one among the English gods. The chief
narrator adds that the gods who pleased the
Indians most, braves and squaws included, 'were
commonly the youngest of us,' which shows that
the human was not quite forgotten in the all-
divine. When the time for sailing came, the
devotees were inconsolable. 'They not only in
a sudden did lose all mirth, joy, glad countenance,
pleasant speeches, agility of body, and all pleasure,
but, with sighs and sorrowings, they poured out
woefull complayntes and moans with bitter tears,
and wringing of their hands, and tormenting of

themselves.' The last the English saw of them was the whole devoted tribe assembled on the hill around a sacrificial fire, whence they implored their gods to bring their heaven back to earth.

From California Drake sailed to the Philippines; and then to the Moluccas, where the Portuguese had, if such a thing were possible, outdone even the Spaniards in their fiendish dealings with the natives. Lopez de Mosquito—viler than his pestilential name — had murdered the Sultan, who was then his guest, chopped up the body, and thrown it into the sea. Baber, the Sultan's son, had driven out the Portuguese from the island of Ternate and was preparing to do likewise from the island of Tidore, when Drake arrived. Baber then offered Drake, for Queen Elizabeth, the complete monopoly of the trade in spices if only Drake would use the *Golden Hind* as the flagship against the Portuguese. Drake's reception was full of Oriental state; and Sultan Baber was so entranced by Drake's musicians that he sat all afternoon among them in a boat towed by the *Golden Hind*. But it was too great a risk to take a hand in this new war with only fifty-six men left. So Drake traded for all the spices he

could stow away and concluded a sort of under-
standing which formed the sheet anchor of English
diplomacy in Eastern seas for another century
to come. Elizabeth was so delighted with this
result that she gave Drake a cup (still at the
family seat of Nutwell Court in Devonshire)
engraved with a picture of his reception by the
Sultan Baber of Ternate.

Leaving Ternate, the *Golden Hind* beat to and
fro among the tortuous and only half-known
channels of the Archipelago till the 9th of January, 1580, when she bore away before a roaring
trade wind with all sail set and, so far as Drake
could tell, a good clear course for home. But
suddenly, without a moment's warning, there
was a most terrific shock. The gallant ship
reared like a stricken charger, plunged forward,
grinding her trembling hull against the rocks,
and then lay pounding out her life upon a reef.
Drake and his men at once took in half the straining sails; then knelt in prayer; then rose to see
what could be done by earthly means. To their
dismay there was no holding ground on which
to get an anchor fast and warp the vessel off.
The lead could find no bottom anywhere aft.
All night long the *Golden Hind* remained fast caught

in this insidious death-trap. At dawn Parson
Fletcher preached a sermon and administered
the Blessed Sacrament. Then Drake ordered
ten tons overboard — cannon, cloves, and provisions. The tide was now low and she sewed seven
feet, her draught being thirteen and the depth of
water only six. Still she kept an even keel as the
reef was to leeward and she had just sail enough
to hold her up. But at high tide in the afternoon
there was a lull and she began to heel over towards the unfathomable depths. Just then,
however, a quiver ran through her from stem to
stern; an extra sail that Drake had ordered up
caught what little wind there was; and, with the
last throb of the rising tide, she shook herself free
and took the water as quietly as if her hull was being launched. There were perils enough to follow:
dangers of navigation, the arrival of a Portuguese fleet that was only just eluded, and all the
ordinary risks of travel in times when what might
be called the official guide to voyagers opened
with the ominous advice, *First make thy Will*.
But the greatest had now been safely passed.

Meanwhile all sorts of rumors were rife in Spain,
New Spain, and England. Drake had been

hanged. That rumor came from the hanging of John Oxenham at Lima. The *Golden Hind* had foundered. That tale was what Winter, captain of the *Elizabeth*, was not altogether unwilling should be thought after his own failure to face another great antarctic storm. He had returned in 1578. News from Peru and Mexico came home in 1579; but no Drake. So, as 1580 wore on, his friends began to despair, the Spaniards and Portuguese rejoiced, while Burleigh, with all who found Drake an inconvenience in their diplomatic way, began to hope that perhaps the sea had smoothed things over. In August the London merchants were thrown into consternation by the report of Drake's incredible captures; for their own merchant fleet was just then off for Spain. They waited on the Council, who soothed them with the assurance that Drake's voyage was a purely private venture so far as prizes were concerned. With this diplomatic quibble they were forced to be content.

But worse was soon to follow. The king of Portugal died. Philip's army marched on Lisbon immediately, and all the Portuguese possessions were added to the already overgrown empire of Spain. Worse still, this annexation gave Philip what he wanted in the way of ships; for Portugal had more than Spain. The Great Armada was now expected to be formed against England, unless Elizabeth's miraculous diplomacy could once more get her clear of the fast-entangling coils. To add to the general confusion, this was also the year in which the Pope sent his picked Jesuits to England, and in which Eliza-beth was carrying on her last great international flirtation with ugly, dissipated Francis of Anjou, brother to the king of France.

Into this imbroglio sailed the *Golden Hind* with ballast of silver and cargo of gold. 'Is Her Majesty alive and well?' said Drake to the first sail outside of Plymouth Sound. 'Ay, ay, she is, my Master,' answered the skipper of a fishing smack, 'but there's a deal o' sickness here in Plymouth'; on which Drake, ready for any excuse to stay afloat, came to anchor in the harbor. His wife, pretty Mary Newman from the banks of Tavy, took boat to see him, as did the Mayor, whose business was to warn him to keep quiet till his course was clear. So Drake wrote off to the Queen and all the Councillors who were on his side. The answer from the Councillors was not encouraging; so he warped out quietly and anchored again behind Drake's Island in the Sound. But presently the Queen's own message came, commanding him to an audience at which, she said, she would be pleased to view some of the curiosities he had brought from foreign parts. Straight on that hint he started up to town with spices, diamonds, pearls, and gold enough to win any woman's pardon and consent.

The audience lasted six hours. Meanwhile the Council sat without any of Drake's supporters and ordered all the treasure to be impounded in the Tower. But Leicester, Walsingham, and Hatton, all members of Drake's syndicate, refused to sign; while Elizabeth herself, the managing director, suspended the order till her further pleasure should be known. The Spanish ambassador 'did burn with passion against Drake.' The Council was distractingly divided. The London merchants trembled for their fleet. But Elizabeth was determined that the blow to Philip should hurt him as much as it could without producing an immediate war; while down among Drake's own West-Countrymen 'the case was clear in sea divinitie,' as similar cases had often been before. Tremayne, a Devonshire magistrate and friend of the syndicate, could hardly find words to express his contentment with Drake, whom he called 'a man of great government, and that by the rules of God and His Book.'

Elizabeth decided to stand by Drake. She claimed, what was true, that he had injured no actual place or person of the King of Spain's, nothing but property afloat, appropriate for reprisals. All England knew the story of Ulua and approved of reprisals in accordance with the spirit of the age. And the Queen had a special grievance about Ireland, where the Spaniards were entrenched in Smerwick, thus adding to the confusion of a rebellion that never quite died down at any time. Philip explained that the Smerwick Spaniards were there as private volunteers. Elizabeth answered that Drake was just the same. The English tide, at all events, was turning in his favor. The indefatigable Stowe, chronicler of London, records that 'the people generally applauded his wonderful long adventures and rich prizes. His name and fame became admirable in all places, the people swarming daily in the streets to behold him, vowing hatred to all that misliked him.'

The *Golden Hind* had been brought round to London, where she was the greatest attraction of the day. Finally, on the 4th of April, 1581, Elizabeth went on board in state, to a banquet 'finer than has ever been seen in England since King Henry VIII,' said the furious Spanish ambassador in his report to Philip. But this was not her chief offence in Spanish eyes. For here, surrounded by her court, and in the presence of an enormous multitude of her enthusiastic subjects, she openly defied the King of Spain. 'He hath demanded Drake's head of me,' she laughed aloud, 'and here I have a gilded sword to strike it off.' With that she bade Drake kneel. Then, handing the sword to Marchaumont, the special envoy of her French suitor, Francis of Anjou, she ordered him to give the accolade. This done, she pronounced the formula of immemorial fame: *I bid thee rise, Sir Francis Drake!*

CHAPTER VIII

DRAKE CLIPS THE WINGS OF SPAIN

FOR three years after Drake had been dubbed
Sir Francis by the Queen he was the hero of
every class of Englishmen but two: the extreme
Roman Catholics, who wanted Mary Queen of
Scots, and the merchants who were doing business
with Portugal and Spain. The Marian opposition
to the general policy of England persisted for a few
years longer. But the merchants who were the
inheritors of centuries of commercial intercourse
with England's new enemies were soon to receive
a shock that completely changed their minds.
They were themselves one of the strongest fac-
tors that made for war in the knotty problem now to be solved at the cannon's mouth
because English trade was seeking new outlets
in every direction and was beating hard against
every door that foreigners shut in its face.
These merchants would not, however, support
the war party till they were forced to, as they

still hoped to gain by other means what only
war could win.

The year that Drake came home (1580) Philip
at last got hold of a sea-going fleet, the eleven big
Portuguese galleons taken when Lisbon fell. With
the Portuguese ships, sailors, and oversea possessions, with more galleons under construction at
Santander in Spain, and with the galleons of the
Indian Guard built by the great Menendez to protect New Spain: with all this performed or promised, Philip began to feel as if the hour was at
hand when he could do to England what she had
done to him.

In 1583 Santa Cruz, the best Spanish admiral
since the death of Menendez, proposed to form the
nucleus of the Great Armada out of the fleet with
which he had just broken down the last vestige of
Portuguese resistance in the Azores. From that day
on, the idea was never dropped. At the same time
Elizabeth discovered the Paris Plot between Mary
and Philip and the Catholics of France, all of whom
were bent on her destruction. England stood to
arms. But false ideas of naval defence were upper-
most in the Queen's Council. No attempt was
made to strike a concentrated blow at the heart of
the enemy's fleet in his own waters. Instead of

this the English ships were carefully divided among
the three squadrons meant to defend the approaches to England, Ireland, and Scotland, because, as the Queen-in-Council sagely remarked,
who could be expected to know what the enemy's
point of attack would be? The fact is that when
wielding the forces of the fleet and army the Queen
and most of her non-combatant councillors never
quite reached that supreme point of view from
which the greatest statesmen see exactly where
civil control ends and civilian interference begins.
Luckily for England, their mistakes were once
more covered up by a turn of the international
kaleidoscope.

No sooner had the immediate danger of a great
combined attack on England passed away than
Elizabeth returned to Drake's plan for a regular
raid against New Spain, though it had to be one
that was not designed to bring on war in Europe.
Drake, who was a member of the Navy Board
charged with the reorganization of the fleet, was
to have command. The ships and men were ready.
But the time had not yet come.

Next year (1584) Amadas and Barlow, Sir
Walter Raleigh's two prospectors for the 'plantation' of Virginia, were being delighted with the

summer lands and waters of what is now North Carolina. We shall soon hear more of Raleigh and his vision of the West. But at this time a good many important events were happening in Europe; and it is these that we must follow first.

William of Orange, the Washington of Holland, was assassinated at Philip's instigation, while plots to kill Elizabeth and place Mary on the throne began to multiply. The agents were executed, while a 'Bond of Association' was signed by all Elizabeth's chief supporters, binding them to hunt down and kill all who tried to kill her—a plain hint for Mary Queen of Scots to stop plotting or stand the consequences.

But the merchants trading with Spain and Portugal were more than ever for keeping on good terms with Philip because the failure of the Spanish harvest had induced him to offer them special protection and encouragement if they would supply his country's needs at once. Every available ton of shipping was accordingly taken up for Spain. The English merchant fleet went out, and big profits seemed assured. But presently the *Primrose*, 'a tall ship of London,' came flying home to say that Philip had suddenly seized the merchandise, imprisoned the men, and taken the ships

and guns for use with the Great Armada.   That
was the last straw.   The peaceful traders now saw
that they were wrong and that the fighting ones
were right; and for the first time both could rejoice
over the clever trick by which John Hawkins had
got his own again from Philip.   In 1571, three
years after Don Martin's treachery at San Juan
de Ulua, Hawkins, while commanding the Scilly
Island squadron, led the Spanish ambassador to
believe that he would go over to the Spanish cause
in Ireland if his claims for damages were only paid
in full and all his surviving men in Mexico were
sent home.   The cold and crafty Philip swallowed
this tempting bait; sent the men home with Spanish dollars in their pockets, and paid Hawkins
forty thousand pounds, the worth of about two
million dollars now.   Then Hawkins used the information he had picked up behind the Spanish
scenes to unravel the Ridolfi Plot for putting
Mary on the throne in 1572, the year of St. Bartholomew.   No wonder Philip hated sea-dogs!

Things new and old having reached this pass,
the whole of England, bar the Marians, were
eager for the great 'Indies Voyage' of 1585.
Londoners crowded down to Woolwich 'with great
jolitie' to see off their own contingent on its way

to join Drake's flag at Plymouth. Very probably Shakespeare went down too, for that famous London merchantman, the *Tiger*, to which he twice alludes—once in *Macbeth* and once in *Twelfth Night*—was off with this contingent. Such a private fleet had never yet been seen: twenty-one ships, eight smart pinnaces, and twenty-three hundred men of every rank and rating. The Queen was principal shareholder and managing director. But, as usual in colonial attacks intended for disavowal if necessity arose, no prospectus or other document was published, nor were the shareholders of this joint-stock company known in any quite official way. It was the size of the fleet and the reputation of the officers that made it a national affair. Drake, now forty, was 'Admiral'; Frobisher, of North-West-Passage fame, was 'Vice'; Knollys, the Queen's own cousin, 'Rear.' Carleill, a famous general, commanded the troops and sailed in Shakespeare's *Tiger*. Drake's old crew from the *Golden Hind* came forward to a man, among them Wright, 'that excellent mathematician and ingineer,' and big Tom Moone, the lion of all boarding-parties, each in command of a ship.

But Elizabeth was just then weaving the threads

of an unusually intricate diplomatic pattern; so doubts and delays, orders and counter-orders vexed Drake to the last. Sir Philip Sidney, too, came down as a volunteer; which was another sore vexation, since his European fame would have made him practically joint commander of the fleet, although he was not a naval officer at all. But he had the good sense to go back; whereupon Drake, fearing further interruptions from the court, ordered everything to be tumbled into the nearest ships and hurried off to sea under a press of sail.

The first port of call was Vigo in the north-western corner of Spain, where Drake's envoy told the astonished governor that Elizabeth wanted to know what Philip intended doing about embargoes now. If the governor wanted peace, he must listen to Drake's arguments; if war — well, Drake was ready to begin at once. A three-days' storm interrupted the proceedings; after which the English intercepted the fugitive townsfolk whose flight showed that the governor meant to make a stand, though he had said the embargo had been lifted and that all the English prisoners were at liberty to go. Some English sailors, however, were still being held; so Drake sent in an armed party and brought them off, with a good pile of reprisal booty too.   Then he put to sea and made for the Spanish Main by way of the Portuguese African islands.

The plan of campaign drawn up for Burleigh's information still exists.   It shows that Drake, the consummate raider, was also an admiral of the highest kind.   The items, showing how long each part should take and what loot each place should yield, are exact and interesting.   But it is in the relation of every part to every other part and to the whole that the original genius of the born commander shines forth in all its glory.   After taking San Domingo he was to sack Margarita, La Hacha, and Santa Marta, razing their fortifications as he left. Cartagena and Nombre de Dios came next.   Then Carleill was to raid Panama, with the help of the Maroons, while Drake himself was to raid the coast of Honduras.   Finally, with reunited forces, he would take Havana and, if possible, hold it by leaving a sufficient garrison behind.   Thus he would paralyze New Spain by destroying all the points of junction along its lines of communication just when Philip stood most in need of its help for completing the Great Armada.

But, like a mettlesome steeplechaser, Drake took

a leap in his stride during the preliminary canter
before the great race. The wind being foul for the
Canaries, he went on to the Cape Verde archipelago
and captured Santiago, which had been abandoned
in terror on the approach of the English 'Dragon,'
that sinister hero of Lope de Vega's epic onslaught
La Dragontea. As good luck would have it, Carleill
marched in on the anniversary of the Queen's accession, the 17th of November. So there was a royal
salute fired in Her Majesty's honor by land and sea.
No treasure was found. French privateers had
sacked the place three years before and had killed
off everyone they caught; the Portuguese, therefore, were not going to wait to meet the English
'Dragon' too. The force that marched inland failed
to unearth the governor. So San Domingo, Santiago, and Porto Praya were all burnt to the ground
before the fleet bore away for the West Indies.

San Domingo in Hispaniola (Hayti) was made
in due course, but only after a virulent epidemic
had seriously thinned the ranks. San Domingo
was the oldest town in New Spain and was strongly
garrisoned and fortified. But Carleill's soldiers
carried all before them. Drake battered down the
seaward walls. The Spaniards abandoned the
citadel at night, and the English took the whole

place as a New Year's gift for 1586. But again there was no treasure. The Spaniards had killed off the Caribs in war or in the mines, so that nothing was now dug out. Moreover the citizens were quite on their guard against adventurers and ready to hide what they had in the most inaccessible places. Drake then put the town up to ransom and sent out his own Maroon boy servant to bring in the message from the Spanish officer proposing terms. This Spaniard, hating all Maroons, ran his lance through the boy and cantered away. The boy came back with the last ounce of his strength and fell dead at Drake's feet. Drake sent to say he would hang two Spaniards every day if the murderer was not hanged by his own compatriots. As no one came he began with two friars. Then the Spaniards brought in the offender and hanged him in the presence of both armies.

That episode cleared the air; and an interchange of courtesies and hospitalities immediately followed. But no business was done. Drake therefore began to burn the town bit by bit till twenty-five thousand ducats were paid. It was very little for the capital. But the men picked up a good deal of loot in the process and vented their ultra-Protestant zeal on all the 'graven images' that

were not worth keeping for sale. On the whole the
English were well satisfied. They had taken all
the Spanish ships and armament they wanted,
destroyed the rest, liberated over a hundred
brawny galley-slaves — some Turks among them —
all anxious for revenge, and had struck a blow at
Spanish prestige which echoed back to Europe.
Spain never hid her light under a bushel; and here,
in the Governor's Palace, was a huge escutcheon
with a horse standing on the earth and pawing at
the sky. The motto blazoned on it was to the effect
that the earth itself was not enough for Spain—*Non
sufficit orbis*. Drake's humor was greatly tickled,
and he and his officers kept asking the Spaniards
to translate the motto again and again.

Delays and tempestuous head winds induced
Drake to let intermediate points alone and make
straight for Cartagena on the South American mainland. Cartagena had been warned and was on the
alert. It was strong by both nature and art. The
garrison was good of its kind, though the Spaniards'
custom of fighting in quilted jackets instead of
armor put them at a disadvantage. This custom
was due to the heat and to the fact that the jackets
were proof against the native arrows.

There was an outer and an inner harbor, with

such an intricate and well-defended passage that no one thought Drake would dare go in. But he did. Frobisher had failed to catch a pilot. But Drake did the trick without one, to the utter dismay of the Spaniards. After some more very clever manœuvres, to distract the enemy's attention from the real point of attack, Carleill and the soldiers landed under cover of the dark and came upon the town where they were least expected, by wading waist-deep through the water just out of sight of the Spanish gunners. The entrenchments did not bar the way in this unexpected quarter. But wine casks full of rammed earth had been hurriedly piled there in case the mad English should make the attempt. Carleill gave the signal. Goring's musketeers sprang forward and fired into the Spaniards' faces. Then Sampson's pikemen charged through and a desperate hand-to-hand fight ensued. Finally the Spaniards broke after Carleill had killed their standard-bearer and Goring had wounded and taken their commander. The enemies ran pell-mell through the town together till the English reformed in the Plaza. Next day Drake moved in to attack the harbor fort; whereupon it was abandoned and the whole place fell.

But again there was a dearth of booty. The Spaniards were getting shy of keeping too many valuables where they could be taken. So negotiations, emphasized by piecemeal destruction, went on till sickness and the lateness of the season put the English in a sorry fix. The sack of the city had yielded much less than that of San Domingo; and the men, who were all volunteers, to be paid out of plunder, began to grumble at their ill-success. Many had been wounded, several killed — big, faithful Tom Moone among them. A hundred died. More were ill. Two councils of war were held, one naval, the other military. The military officers agreed to give up all their own shares to the men. But the naval officers, who were poorer and who were also responsible for the expenses of their vessels, could not concur. Finally 110,000 ducats (equivalent in purchasing power to nearly three millions of dollars) were accepted.

It was now impossible to complete the programme or even to take Havana, in view of the renewed sickness, the losses, and the advance of the season. A further disappointment was experienced when Drake just missed the treasure fleet by only half a day, though through no fault of his own. Then, with constantly diminishing

numbers of effective men, the course was shaped
for the Spanish 'plantation' of St. Augustine in
Florida. This place was utterly destroyed and
some guns and money were taken from it. Then
the fleet stood north again till, on the 9th of June,
it found Raleigh's colony of Roanoke.

Ralph Lane, the governor, was in his fort on the
island ready to brave it out. Drake offered a free
passage home to all the colonists. But Lane preferred staying and going on with his surveys and
'plantation.' Drake then filled up a store ship to
leave behind with Lane. But a terrific three-day
storm wrecked the store ship and damped the
colonists' enthusiasm so much that they persuaded
Lane to change his mind. The colonists embarked
and the fleet then bore away for home. Though
balked of much it had expected in the way of
booty, reduced in strength by losses, and therefore
unable to garrison any strategic point which would
threaten the life of New Spain, its purely naval
work was a true and glorious success. When he
arrived at Plymouth, Drake wrote immediately to
Burleigh: 'My very good Lord, there is now a very
great gap opened, very little to the liking of the
King of Spain.'

This 'very great gap' on the American side of

the Atlantic was soon to be matched by the still
greater gap Drake was to make on the European
side by destroying the Spanish Armada and
thus securing that mightiest of ocean highways
through which the hosts of emigration afterwards
poured into a land endowed with the goodly
heritage of English liberty and the English tongue.

The year of Drake's return (1586) was no less
troublous than its immediate predecessors. The
discovery of the Babington Plot to assassinate
Elizabeth and to place Mary on the throne, sup-
ported by Scotland, France, and Spain, proved
Mary's complicity, produced an actual threat of
war from France, and made the Pope and Philip
gnash their teeth with rage. The Roman Catholic
allied powers had no sufficient navy, and Philip's
credit was at its lowest ebb after Drake's devastat-
ing raid. The English were exultant, east and
west; for the *True Report of a Worthie Fight performed in the voiage from Turkie by Five Shippes of
London against 11 gallies and two frigats of the King
of Spain at Pantalarea, within the Straits* [of Gib-
raltar] *Anno 1586* was going the rounds and
running a close second to Drake's West India
achievement. The ignorant and thoughtless, both

then and since, mistook this fight, and another like it in 1590, to mean that English merchantmen could beat off Spanish men-of-war. Nothing of the kind: the English Levanters were heavily armed and admirably manned by well-trained fighting crews; and what these actions really proved, if proof was necessary, was that galleys were no match for broadsides from the proper kind of sailing ships.

Turkey came into the problems of 1586 in more than name, for there was a vast diplomatic scheme on foot to unite the Turks with such Portuguese as would support Antonio, the pretender to the throne of Portugal, and the rebellious Dutch against Spain, Catholic France, and Mary Stuart's Scotland. Leicester was in the Netherlands with an English army, fighting indecisively, losing Sir Philip Sidney and angering Elizabeth by accepting the governor-generalship without her leave and against her diplomacy, which, now as ever, was opposed to any definite avowal that could possibly be helped.

Meanwhile the Great Armada was working up its strength, and Drake was commissioned to weaken it as much as possible. But, on the 8th of February, 1587, before he could sail, Mary was at last beheaded, and Elizabeth was once more entering on a tricky course of tortuous diplomacy too long by half to follow here. As the great crisis approached, it had become clearer and clearer that it was a case of kill or be killed between Elizabeth and Mary, and that England could not afford to leave Marian enemies in the rear when there might be a vast Catholic alliance in the front. But, as a sovereign, Elizabeth disliked the execution of any crowned head; as a wily woman she wanted to make the most of both sides; and as a diplomatist she would not have open war and direct operations going down to the root of the evil if devious ways would do.

So the peace party of the Council prevailed again, and Drake's orders were changed. He had been going as a lion. The peace party now tried to send him as a fox. But he stretched his instructions to their utmost limits and even defied the custom of the service by holding no council of war when deciding to swoop on Cadiz.

As they entered the harbor, the English saw sixty ships engaged in preparations for the Great Armada. Many had no sails—to keep the crews from deserting. Others were waiting for their guns to come from Italy. Ten galleys rowed out to protect them. The weather and surroundings were perfect for these galleys. But as they came end-on in line-abreast Drake crossed their T in line-ahead with the shattering broadsides of four Queen's ships which soon sent them flying. Each galley was the upright of the T, each English sailing ship the corresponding cross-piece. Then Drake attacked the shipping and wrecked it right and left. Next morning he led the pinnaces and boats into the inner harbor, where they cut out the big galleon belonging to Santa Cruz himself, the Spanish commander-in-chief. Then the galleys got their chance again—an absolutely perfect chance, because Drake's fleet was becalmed at the very worst possible place for sailing ships and the very best possible place for the well-oared galleys. But even under these extraordinary circumstances the ships smashed the galleys up with broadside fire and sent them back to cover. Then the Spaniards towed some fire-ships out. But the English rowed for them, threw grappling irons into them, and gave them a turn that took them clear. Then, for the last time, the galleys came on, as bravely but as uselessly as ever. When Drake sailed away he left the shipping of Cadiz completely out of action for months to come, though fifteen sail escaped destruction in the inner harbor. His own losses were quite insignificant.

The next objective was Cape St. Vincent, so famous through centuries of naval history because it is the great strategic salient thrust out into the Atlantic from the southwest corner of Europe, and thus commands the flank approaches to and from the Mediterranean, to and from the coast of Africa, and, in those days, the route to and from New Spain by way of the Azores. Here Drake had trouble with Borough, his second-in-command, a friend of cautious Burleigh and a man hide-bound in the warfare of the past—a sort of English Don. Borough objected to Drake's taking decisive action without the vote of a council of war. Remembering the terrors of Italian textbooks, he had continued to regard the galleys with much respect in the harbor of Cadiz even after Drake had broken them with ease. Finally, still clinging to the old ways of mere raids and reprisals, he stood aghast at the idea of seizing Cape St. Vincent and making it a base of operations. Drake promptly put him under arrest.

Sagres Castle, commanding the roadstead of Cape St. Vincent, was extraordinarily strong. The cliffs, on which it occupied about a hundred acres, rose sheer two hundred feet all round except at a narrow and well defended neck only two hundred yards across. Drake led the stormers himself. While half his eight hundred men kept up a continuous fire against every Spaniard on the wall the other half rushed piles of faggots in against the oak and iron gate. Drake was foremost in this work, carrying faggots himself and applying the first match. For two hours the fight went on; when suddenly the Spaniards sounded a parley. Their commanding officer had been killed and the woodwork of the gate had taken fire. In those days a garrison that would not surrender was put to the sword when captured; so these Spaniards may well be excused. Drake willingly granted them the honors of war; and so, even to his own surprise, the castle fell without another blow. The minor forts near by at once surrendered and were destroyed, while the guns of Sagres were thrown over the cliffs and picked up by the men below. The whole neighboring coast was then swept clear of the fishing fleet which was the main source of supply used for the Great Armada.

The next objective was Lisbon, the headquarters of the Great Armada, one of the finest harbors in the world, and then the best fortified of all. Tak-

ing it was, of course, out of the question without
a much larger fleet accompanied by an overwhelming army. But Drake reconnoitred to good effect,
learnt wrinkles that saved him from disaster two
years later, and retired after assuring himself that
an Armada which could not fight him then could
never get to England during the same season.

Ship fevers and all the other epidemics that
dogged the old sailing fleets and scourged them
like the plague never waited long. Drake was
soon short-handed. To add to his troubles, Borough sailed away for home; whereupon Drake
tried him and his officers by court-martial and
condemned them all to death. This penalty was
never carried out, for reasons we shall soon understand. Since no reinforcements came from home,
Cape St. Vincent could not be held any longer.
There was, however, one more stroke to make.
The great East-India Spanish treasure ship was
coming home; and Drake made up his mind to
have her.

Off the Azores he met her coming towards him
and dipping her colors again and again to ask him
who he was. 'But we would put out no flag till
we were within shot of her, when we hanged out
flags, streamers, and pendants. Which done, we

haiied her with cannon-shot; and having shot her through divers times, she shot at us. Then we began to ply her hotly, our fly boat [lightly armed supply vessel of comparatively small size] and one of our pinnaces lying athwart her hawse [across her bows] at whom she shot and threw fire-works [incendiary missiles] but did them no hurt, in that her ordnance lay so high over them. Then she, seeing us ready to lay her aboard [range up alongside], all of our ships plying her so hotly, and resolutely determined to make short work of her, they yielded to us.' The Spaniards fought bravely, as they generally did. But they were only naval amateurs compared with the trained professional sea-dogs.

The voyage was now 'made' in the old sense of that term; for this prize was 'the greatest ship in all Portugal, richly laden, to our Happy Joy.' The relative values, then and now, are impossible to fix, because not only was one dollar the equivalent in most ways of ten dollars now but, in view of the smaller material scale on which men's lives were lived, these ten dollars might themselves be multiplied by ten, or more, without producing the same effect as the multiplied sum would now produce on international affairs. Suffice it to say

that the ship was worth nearly five million dollars
of actual cash, and ten, twenty, thirty, or many
more millions if present sums of money are to be
considered relatively to the national incomes of
those poorer days.

But better than spices, jewels, and gold were
the secret documents which revealed the dazzling
profits of the new East-India trade by sea. From
that time on for the next twelve years the London
merchants and their friends at court worked steadily for official sanction in this most promising direction. At last, on the 31st of December, 1600, the
documents captured by Drake produced their
result, and the East-India Company, by far the
greatest corporation of its kind the world has ever
seen, was granted a royal charter for exclusive
trade. Drake may therefore be said not only to
have set the course for the United States but to
have actually discovered the route leading to the
Empire of India, now peopled by three hundred
million subjects of the British Crown.

So ended the famous campaign of 1587, popu-
larly known as the singeing of King Philip's beard.
Beyond a doubt it was the most consummate
work of naval strategy which, up to that time, all
history records.

CHAPTER IX

WITH 1588 the final crisis came. Philip —
haughty, gloomy, and ambitious Philip, unskilled
in arms, but persistent in his plans — sat in his
palace at Madrid like a spider forever spinning
webs that enemies tore down. Drake and the
English had thrown the whole scheme of the
Armada's mobilization completely out of gear.
Philip's well-intentioned orders and counter-
orders had made confusion worse confounded; and
though the Spanish empire held half the riches of
the world it felt the lack of ready money because
English sea power had made it all parts and no
whole for several months together. Then, when
mobilization was resumed, Philip found himself
distracted by expert advice from Santa Cruz, his
admiral, and from Parma, Alva's successor in the
Netherlands.

The general idea was to send the Invincible

172

Armada up the English Channel as far as the Netherlands, where Parma would be ready with a magnificent Spanish army waiting aboard troopships for safe conduct into England. The Spanish regulars could then hold London up to ransom or burn it to the ground. So far, so good. But Philip, to whom amphibious warfare remained an unsolved mystery, thought that the Armada and the Spanish army could conquer England without actually destroying the English fleet. He could not see where raids must end and conquest must begin. Most Spaniards agreed with him. Parma and Santa Cruz did not. Parma, as a very able general, wanted to know how his oversea communications could be made quite safe. Santa Cruz, as a very able admiral, knew that no such sea road could possibly be safe while the ubiquitous English navy was undefeated and at large. Some time or other a naval battle must be won, or Parma's troops, cut off from their base of supplies and surrounded like an island by an angry sea of enemies, must surely perish. Win first at sea and then on land, said the expert warriors, Santa Cruz and Parma. Get into hated England with the least possible fighting, risk, or loss, said the mere politician, Philip, and then crush Drake if he annoys you.

Early and late persistent Philip slaved away upon this 'Enterprize of England.' With incredible toil he spun his web anew. The ships were collected into squadrons; the squadrons at last began to wear the semblance of a fleet. But semblance only. There were far too many soldiers and not nearly enough sailors. Instead of sending the fighting fleet to try to clear the way for the troopships coming later on, Philip mixed army and navy together. The men-of-war were not bad of their kind; but the kind was bad. They were floating castles, high out of the water, crammed with soldiers, some other landsmen, and stores, and with only light ordnance, badly distributed so as to fire at rigging and superstructures only, not at the hulls as the English did. Yet this was not the worst. The worst was that the fighting fleet was cumbered with troopships which might have been useful in boarding, but which were perfectly useless in fighting of any other kind — and the English men-of-war were much too handy to be laid aboard by the lubberly Spanish troopships. Santa Cruz worked himself to death. In one of his last dispatches he begged for more and better guns. All Philip could do was to authorize the purchase of whatever guns the foreign merchantmen in Lisbon harbor could be induced to sell. Sixty second-rate pieces were obtained in this way.

Then, worn out by work and worry, Santa Cruz died, and Philip forced the command on a most reluctant landlubber, the Duke of Medina Sidonia, a very great grandee of Spain, but wholly unfitted to lead a fleet. The death of Santa Cruz, in whom the fleet and army had great confidence, nearly upset the whole 'Enterprize of England.' The captains were as unwilling to serve under bandy-legged, sea-sick Sidonia as he was unwilling to command them. Volunteering ceased. Compulsion failed to bring in the skilled ratings urgently required. The sailors were now not only fewer than ever — sickness and desertion had been thinning their ranks — but many of these few were unfit for the higher kinds of seamanship, while only the merest handful of them were qualified as seamen gunners. Philip, however, was determined; and so the doomed Armada struggled on, fitting its imperfect parts together into a still more imperfect whole until, in June, it was as ready as it ever could be made.

Meanwhile the English had their troubles too. These were also political. But the English navy was of such overwhelming strength that it could stand them with impunity. The Queen, after thirty years of wonderful, if tortuous, diplomacy, was still disinclined to drop the art in which she was supreme for that in which she counted for so much less and by which she was obliged to spend so very much more. There was still a little peace party also bent on diplomacy instead of war. Negotiations were opened with Parma at Flushing and diplomatic 'feelers' went out towards Philip, who sent back some of his own. But the time had come for war. The stream was now too strong for either Elizabeth or Philip to stem or even divert into minor channels.

Lord Howard of Effingham, as Lord High Admiral of England, was charged with the defence at sea. It was impossible in those days to have any great force without some great nobleman in charge of it, because the people still looked on such men as their natural viceroys and commanders. But just as Sir John Norreys, the most expert professional soldier in England, was made Chief of the Staff to the Earl of Leicester ashore, so Drake was made Chief of the Staff to Howard afloat, which meant that he was the brain of the fleet.

A directing brain was sadly needed — not that brains were lacking, but that some one man of original and creative genius was required to bring the modern naval system into triumphant being. Like all political heads, Elizabeth was sensitive to public opinion; and public opinion was ignorant enough to clamor for protection by something that a man could see; besides which there were all those weaklings who have been described as the old women of both sexes and all ages, and who have always been the nuisance they are still. Adding together the old views of warfare, which nearly everybody held, and the human weaknesses we have always with us, there was a most dangerously strong public opinion in favor of dividing up the navy so as to let enough different places actually see that they had some visible means of divided defence.

The 30th of March, 1588, is the day of days to be remembered in the history of sea power because it was then that Drake, writing from Plymouth to the Queen-in-Council, first formulated the true doctrine of modern naval warfare, especially the cardinal principle that the best of all defence is to attack your enemy's main fleet as it issues from its ports. This marked the birth of the system perfected by Nelson and thence passed on, with many new developments, to the British Grand Fleet in

12

the Great War of to-day. The first step was by
far the hardest, for Drake had to convert the Queen
and Howard to his own revolutionary views. He
at last succeeded; and on the 7th of July sailed for
Corunna, where the Armada had rendezvoused
after being dispersed by a storm.

Every man afloat knew that the hour had come.
Yet Elizabeth, partly on the score of expense,
partly not to let Drake snap her apron-strings
completely, had kept the supply of food and even
of ammunition very short; so much so that Drake
knew he would have to starve or else replenish from
the Spanish fleet itself. As he drew near Corunna
on the 8th, the Spaniards were again reorganizing.
Hundreds of perfectly useless landlubbers, shipped
at Lisbon to complete the absurdly undermanned
ships, were being dismissed at Corunna. On the
9th, when Sidonia assembled a council of war to
decide whether to put to sea or not, the English
van was almost in sight of the coast. But then
the north wind flawed, failed, and at last chopped
round. A roaring sou'wester came on; and the
great strategic move was over.

On the 12th the fleet was back in Plymouth
replenishing as hard as it could. Howard behaved
to perfection. Drake worked the strategy and

tactics. But Howard had to set the tone, afloat and ashore, to all who came within his sphere of influence; and right well he set it. His dispatches at this juncture are models of what such documents should be; and their undaunted confidence is in marked contrast to what the doomed Spanish officers were writing at the selfsame time.

The southwest wind that turned Drake back brought the Armada out and gave it an advantage which would have been fatal to England had the fleets been really equal, or the Spaniards in superior strength, for a week was a very short time in which to replenish the stores that Elizabeth had purposely kept so low. Drake and Howard, so the story goes, were playing a game of bowls on Plymouth Hoe on Friday afternoon the 19th of July when Captain Fleming of the *Golden Hind* rushed up to say the Spanish fleet was off the Lizard, only sixty miles away! All eyes turned to Drake. Divining the right way to calm the people, he whispered an order and then said out loud: 'There's time to end our game and beat the Spaniards too.' The shortness of food and ammunition that had compelled him to come back instead of waiting to blockade now threatened to get him nicely caught in the very trap he had wished to catch the Great Armada in himself; for the Spaniards, coming up with the wind, might catch him struggling out against the wind and crush his long emerging column, bit by bit, precisely as he had intended crushing their own column as it issued from the Tagus or Corunna.

But it was only the van that Fleming had sighted. Many a Spanish straggler was still hull-down astern; and Sidonia had to wait for all to close and form up properly.

Meanwhile Drake and Howard were straining every nerve to get out of Plymouth. It was not their fault, but the Queen's-in-Council, that Sidonia had unwittingly stolen this march on them. It was their glory that they won the lost advantage back again. All afternoon and evening, all through that summer night, the sea-dog crews were warping out of harbor. Torches, flares, and cressets threw their fitful light on toiling lines of men hauling on ropes that moved the ships apparently like snails. But once in Plymouth Sound the whinnying sheaves and long *yo-hoes!* told that all the sail the ships could carry was being made for a life-or-death effort to win the weather gage. Thus beat the heart of naval England that momentous night in Plymouth Sound, while beacons blazed from height to height ashore, horsemen spurred off post-haste with orders and dispatches, and every able-bodied landsman stood to arms.

Next morning Drake was in the Channel, near the Eddystone, with fifty-four sail, when he sighted a dim blur to windward through the thickening mist and drizzling rain. This was the Great Armada. Rain came on and killed the wind. All sail was taken in aboard the English fleet, which lay under bare poles, invisible to the Spaniards, who still announced their presence with some show of canvas.

In actual size and numbers the Spaniards were superior at first. But as the week-long running fight progressed the English evened up with reinforcements. Spanish vessels looked bigger than their tonnage, being high built; and Spanish official reports likewise exaggerated the size because their system of measurement made their three tons equal to an English four. In armament and seamen-gunners the English were perhaps five times as strong as the Armada — and seamen-gunners won the day. The English seamen greatly outnumbered the Spanish seamen, utterly surpassed them in seamanship, and enjoyed the further advantage of having far handier vessels to work.

The Spanish grand total, for all ranks and ratings, was thirty thousand men; the English, only fifteen. But the Spaniards were six thousand short on arrival; and their actual seamen, many of whom were only half-trained, then numbered a bare seven thousand. The seventeen thousand soldiers only made the ships so many death-traps; for they were of no use afloat except as boarding parties — and no boarding whatever took place. The English fifteen thousand, on the other hand, were three-quarters seamen and one-quarter soldiers who were mostly trained as marines, and this total was actually present. On the whole, it is hardly an exaggeration to say that the Armada was mostly composed of armed transports while all the English vessels that counted in the fighting were real men-of-war.

In every one of the Armada's hundred and twenty-eight vessels, says an officer of the Spanish flagship, 'our people kneeled down and offered a prayer, beseeching our Lord to give us victory against the enemies of His holy faith.' The crews of the hundred and ninety-seven English vessels which, at one time or another, were present in some capacity on the scene of action also prayed for victory to the Lord of Hosts, but took the

proper naval means to win it. 'Trust in the Lord
— and keep your powder dry,' said Oliver Cromwell when about to ford a river in the presence of
the enemy. And so, in other words, said Drake.

All day long, on that fateful 20th of July, the
visible Armada with its swinging canvas was lying-
to fifteen miles west of the invisible, bare-masted
English fleet. Sidonia held a council of war,
which, landsman-like, believed that the English
were divided, one-half watching Parma, the other
the Armada. The trained soldiers and sailors
were for the sound plan of attacking Plymouth
first. Some admirals even proposed the only perfect plan of crushing Drake in detail as he issued
from the Sound. All were in blissful ignorance of
the astounding feat of English seamanship which
had already robbed them of the only chance they
ever had. But Philip, also landsman-like, had
done his best to thwart his own Armada; for
Sidonia produced the royal orders forbidding any
attack on England till he and Parma had joined
hands. Drake, however, might be crushed piecemeal in the offing when still with his aftermost
ships in the Sound. So, with this true idea, unworkable because based on false information, the
generals and admirals dispersed to their vessels and

waited. But then, just as night was closing in, the weather lifted enough to reveal Drake's astonishing position. Immediately pinnaces went scurrying to Sidonia for orders. But he had none to give. At one in the morning he learnt some more dumbfounding news: that the English had nearly caught him at Corunna, that Drake and Howard had joined forces, and that both were now before him.

Nor was even this the worst. For while the distracted Sidonia was getting his fleet into the 'eagle formation,' so suitable for galleys whose only fighting men were soldiers, the English fleet was stealing the weather gage, his one remaining natural advantage. An English squadron of eight sail manœuvred coast-wise on the Armada's inner flank, while, unperceived by the Spanish lookout, Drake stole away to sea, beat round its outer flank, and then, making the most of a westerly slant in the shifting breeze, edged in to starboard. The Spaniards saw nothing till it was too late, Drake having given them a berth just wide enough to keep them quiet. But when the sun rose, there, only a few miles off to windward, was the whole main body of the English fleet, coming on in faultless line-ahead, heeling nicely over on the port tack before the freshening breeze, and, far from waiting for the Great Armada, boldly bearing down to the attack. With this consummate move the victory was won.

The rest was slaughter, borne by the Spaniards with a resolution that nothing could surpass. With dauntless tenacity they kept their 'eagle formation,' so useful at Lepanto, through seven dire days of most one-sided fighting. Whenever occasion seemed to offer, the Spaniards did their best to close, to grapple, and to board, as had their heroes at Lepanto. But the English merely laughed, ran in, just out of reach, poured in a shattering broadside between wind and water, stood off to reload, fired again, with equal advantage, at longer range, caught the slow galleons end-on, raked them from stem to stern, passed to and fro in one, long, deadly line-ahead, concentrating at will on any given target; and did all this with well-nigh perfect safety to themselves. In quite a different way close-to, but to the same effect at either distance, long or short, the English 'had the range of them,' as sailors say to-day. Close-to, the little Spanish guns fired much too high to hull the English vessels, lying low and trim upon the water, with whose changing humors their lines fell in so much more happily than those of any lumbering Spaniards could. Far-off, the little Spanish guns did correspondingly small damage, even when they managed to hit; while the heavy metal of the English, handled by real seamen-gunners, inflicted crushing damage in return.

But even more important than the Englishmen's superiority in rig, hull, armament, and expert seamanship was their tactical use of the thoroughly modern line-ahead. Any one who will take the letter T as an illustration can easily understand the advantage of 'crossing his T.' The upright represents an enemy caught when in column-ahead, as he would be, for instance, when issuing from a narrow-necked port. In this formation he can only use bow fire, and that only in succession, on a very narrow front. But the fleet represented by the crosspiece, moving across the point of the upright, is in the deadly line-ahead, with all its near broadsides turned in one long converging line of fire against the helplessly narrow-fronted enemy. If the enemy, sticking to mediæval tactics, had room to broaden his front by forming column-abreast, as galleys always did, that is, with several uprights side by side, he would still be at the same sort of disadvantage; for this would only mean a series of T's with each nearest broadside crossing each opposing upright as before.

The herded soldiers and non-combatants aboard the Great Armada stood by their useless duties to the last. Thousands fell killed or wounded. Several times the Spanish scuppers actually ran a horrid red, as if the very ships were bleeding. The priests behaved as bravely as the Jesuits of New France — and who could be braver than those undaunted missionaries were? Soldiers and sailors were alike. 'What shall we do now?' asked Sidonia after the slaughter had gone on for a week. 'Order up more powder,' said Oquendo, as dauntless as before. Even then the eagle formation was still kept up. The van ships were the head. The biggest galleons formed the body. Lighter vessels formed the wings. A reserve formed the tail.

As the unflinching Armada stood slowly up the Channel a sail or two would drop out by the way, dead-beat. One night several strange sail passed suddenly by Drake. What should he do? To go about and follow them with all astern of him doing the same in succession was not to be thought of, as his aftermost vessels were merchantmen, wholly untrained to the exact combined manœuvres required in a fighting fleet, though first-rate individ-

ually.   There was then no night signal equivalent
to the modern 'Disregard the flagship's move-
ments.'   So Drake dowsed his stern light, went
about, overhauled the strangers, and found they
were bewildered German merchantmen.   He had
just gone about once more to resume his own station when suddenly a Spanish flagship loomed up
beside his own flagship the *Revenge*.   Drake immediately had his pinnace lowered away to demand
instant surrender.   But the Spanish admiral was
Don Pedro de Valdes, a very gallant commander
and a very proud grandee, who demanded terms;
and, though his flagship (which had been in colli-
sion with a run-amuck) seemed likely to sink, he
was quite ready to go down fighting.   Yet the
moment he heard that his summoner was Drake he
surrendered at discretion, feeling it a personal
honor, according to the ideas of the age, to yield
his sword to the greatest seaman in the world.
With forty officers he saluted Drake, compliment-
ing him on 'valour and felicity so great that Mars
and Neptune seemed to attend him, as also on his
generosity towards the fallen foe, a quality often
experienced by the Spaniards; whereupon,' adds
this eyewitness, 'Sir Francis Drake, requiting his
Spanish compliments with honest English courte-

sies, placed him at his own table and lodged him in his own cabin.' Drake's enemies at home accused him of having deserted his fleet to capture a treasure ship — for there was a good deal of gold with Valdes. But the charge was quite unfounded.

A very different charge against Howard had more foundation. The Armada had anchored at Calais to get its breath before running the gauntlet for the last time and joining Parma in the Netherlands. But in the dead of night, when the flood was making and a strong west wind was blowing in the same direction as the swirling tidal stream, nine English fire-ships suddenly burst into flame and made for the Spanish anchorage. There were no boats ready to grapple the fire-ships and tow them clear. There was no time to weigh; for every vessel had two anchors down. Sidonia, enraged that the boats were not out on patrol, gave the order for the whole fleet to cut their cables and make off for their lives. As the great lumbering hulls, which had of course been riding head to wind, swung round in the dark and confusion, several crashing collisions occurred. Next morning the Armada was strung along the Flemish coast in disorderly flight. Seeing the impossibility of bringing the leewardly vessels back against the wind in time to form up, Sidonia ran down with the windward ones and formed farther off. Howard then led in pursuit. But seeing the *capitana* of the renowned Italian galleasses in distress near Calais, he became a mediæval knight again, left his fleet, and took the galleasse. For the moment that one feather in his cap seemed better worth having than a general victory.

Drake forged ahead and led the pursuit in turn. The Spaniards fought with desperate courage, still suffering ghastly losses. But, do what they could to bear up against the English and the wind, they were forced to leeward of Dunkirk, and so out of touch with Parma. This was the result of the Battle of Gravelines, fought on Monday the 29th of July, 1588, just ten days after Captain Fleming had rushed on to the bowling green of Plymouth Hoe where Drake and Howard, their shore work done, were playing a game before embarking. In those ten days the gallant Armada had lost all chance of winning the overlordship of the sea and shaking the sea-dog grip off both Americas. A rising gale now forced it to choose between getting pounded to death on the shoals of Dunkirk or running north, through that North Sea in which the British Grand Fleet of the twentieth century fought against the fourth attempt in modern times to win a world-dominion.

North, and still north, round by the surf-lashed Orkneys, then down the wild west coasts of the Hebrides and Ireland, went the forlorn Armada, losing ships and men at every stage, until at last the remnant straggled into Spanish ports like the mere wreckage of a storm.

CHAPTER X

'THE ONE AND THE FIFTY-THREE'

THE next year, 1589, is famous for the unsuccessful Lisbon Expedition. Drake had the usual troubles with Elizabeth, who wanted him to go about picking leaves and breaking branches before laying the axe to the root of the tree. Though there were in the Narrow Seas defensive squadrons strong enough to ward off any possible blow, yet the nervous landsmen wanted Corunna and other ports attacked and their shipping destroyed, for fear England should be invaded before Drake could strike his blow at Lisbon. Then there were troubles about stores and ammunition. The English fleet had been reduced to the last pound of powder twice during the ten-days' battle with the Armada. Yet Elizabeth was again alarmed at the expense of munitions. She never quite rose to the idea of one supreme and finishing blow, no matter what the cost might be.

This was a joint expedition, the first in which a really modern English fleet and army had ever taken part, with Sir John Norreys in command of the army. There was no trouble about recruits, for all men of spirit flocked in to follow Drake and Norreys. The fleet was perfectly organized into appropriate squadrons and flotillas, such as then corresponded with the battleships, cruisers, and mosquito craft of modern navies. The army was organized into battalions and brigades, with a regular staff and all the proper branches of the service.

The fleet made for Corunna, where Norreys won a brilliant victory. A curious little incident of exact punctilio is worth recording. After the battle, and when the fleet was waiting for a fair wind to get out of the harbor, the ships were much annoyed by a battery on the heights. Norreys undertook to storm the works and sent in the usual summons by a *parlementaire* accompanied by a drummer. An angry Spaniard fired from the walls and the drummer fell dead. The English had hostages on whom to take reprisals. But the Spaniards were too quick for them. Within ten minutes the guilty man was tried inside the fort by drum-head court-martial, condemned to death,

and swung out neatly from the walls, while a polite
Spanish officer came over to assure the English
troops that such a breach of discipline should not
occur again.

Lisbon was a failure. The troops landed and
marched over the ground north of Lisbon where
Wellington in a later day made works whose fame
has caused their memory to become an allusion in
English literature for any impregnable base — the
Lines of Torres Vedras. The fleet and the army
now lost touch with each other; and that was the
ruin of them all. Norreys was persuaded by Don
Antonio, pretender to the throne of Portugal which
Philip had seized, to march farther inland, where
Portuguese patriots were said to be ready to rise
en masse. This Antonio was a great talker and a
first-rate fighter with his tongue. But his Portuguese followers, also great talkers, wanted to see
a victory won by arms before they rose.

Before leaving Lisbon Drake had one stroke of
good luck. A Spanish convoy brought in a Han-
seatic Dutch and German fleet of merchantmen
loaded down with contraband of war destined for
Philip's new Armada. Drake swooped on it
immediately and took sixty well-found ships.
Then he went west to the Azores, looking for what

he called 'some comfortable little dew of Heaven,' that is, of course, more prizes of a richer kind. But sickness broke out. The men died off like flies. Storms completed the discomfiture. And the expedition got home with a great deal less than half its strength in men and not enough in value to pay for its expenses. It was held to have failed; and Drake lost favor.

With the sun of Drake's glory in eclipse at court and with Spain and England resting from warfare on the grander scale, there were no more big battles the following year. But the year after that, 1591, is rendered famous in the annals of the sea by Sir Richard Grenville's fight in Drake's old flagship, the *Revenge*. This is the immortal battle of 'the one and the fifty-three' from which Raleigh's prose and Tennyson's verse have made a glory of the pen fit to match the glory of the sword.

Grenville had sat, with Drake and Sir Philip Sidney, on the Parliamentary committee which recommended the royal charter granted to Sir Walter Raleigh for the founding of the first English colony in what is now the United States. Grenville's grandfather, Marshal of Calais to Henry VIII, had the faculty of rhyme, and, in a set of verses very popular in their own day, showed what the Grenville family ambitions were.

> Who seeks the way to win renown,
> Or flies with wings to high desire,
> Who seeks to wear the laurel crown,
> Or hath the mind that would aspire —
> Let him his native soil eschew,
> Let him go range and seek a new.

Grenville himself was a wild and roving blade, no great commander, but an adventurer of the most daring kind by land or sea. He rather enjoyed the consternation he caused by aping the airs of a pirate king. He had a rough way with him at all times; and Ralph Lane was much set against his being the commander of the 'Virginia Voyage' of which Lane himself was the governor on land. But in action he always was, beyond a doubt, the very *beau idéal* of a 'first-class fighting man.' A striking instance of his methods was afforded on his return from Virginia, when he found an armed Spanish treasure ship ahead of him at sea. He had no boat to board her with. But he knocked some sort of one together out of the ship's chests and sprang up the Spaniard's side with his boarding party just as this makeshift boat was sinking under them.

The last fight of the *Revenge* is almost incredible from the odds engaged — fifty-three vessels to one. But it is true; and neither Raleigh's glowing prose nor Tennyson's glowing verse exaggerates it. Lord Thomas Howard, 'almost famished for want of prey,' had been cruising in search of treasure ships when Captain Middleton, one of the gentlemen-adventurers who followed the gallant Earl of Cumberland, came in to warn him that Don Alonzo de Bazan was following with fifty-three sail. The English crews were partly ashore at the Azores; and Howard had barely time to bring them off, cut his cables, and work to windward of the overwhelming Spaniards.

Grenville's men were last. The *Revenge* had only 'her hundred fighters on deck and her ninety sick below' when the Spanish fleet closed round him. Yet, just as he had sworn to cut down the first man who touched a sail when the master thought there was still a chance to slip through, so now he refused to surrender on any terms at all. Then, running down close-hauled on the starboard tack, decks cleared for action and crew at battle quarters, he steered right between two divisions of the Spanish fleet till 'the mountain-like *San Felipe*, of fifteen hundred tons,' ranging up on his weather side, blanketed his canvas and left him almost becalmed. Immediately the vessels which the *Revenge* had weathered hauled their wind and came up on her from to-leeward. Then, at three o'clock in the afternoon of the 1st of September, 1591, that immortal fight began.

The first broadside from the *Revenge* took the *San Felipe* on the water-line and forced her to give way and stop her leaks. Then two Spaniards ranged up in her place, while two more kept station on the other side. And so the desperate fight went on all through that afternoon and evening and far on into the night. Meanwhile Howard, still keeping the weather gage, attacked the Spaniards from the rear and thought of trying to cut through them. But his sailing master swore it would be the end of all Her Majesty's ships engaged, as it probably would; so he bore away, wisely or not as critics may judge for themselves. One vessel, the little *George Noble* of London, a victualler, stood by the *Revenge*, offering help before the fight began. But Grenville, thanking her gallant skipper, ordered him to save his vessel by following Howard.

With never less than one enemy on each side of her, the *Revenge* fought furiously on. *Boarders away!* shouted the Spanish colonels as the vessels closed. *Repel boarders!* shouted Grenville in reply. And they did repel them, time and again, till the English pikes dripped red with Spanish blood. A few Spaniards gained the deck, only to be shot, stabbed, or slashed to death. Towards midnight Grenville was hit in the body by a musket-shot fired from the tops—the same sort of shot that killed Nelson. The surgeon was killed while dressing the wound, and Grenville was hit in the head. But still the fight went on. The *Revenge* had already sunk two Spaniards, a third sank afterwards, and a fourth was beached to save her. But Grenville would not hear of surrender. When day broke not ten unwounded Englishmen remained. The pikes were broken. The powder was spent. The whole deck was a wild entanglement of masts, spars, sails, and rigging. The undaunted survivors stood dumb as their silent cannon. But every Spanish hull in the whole encircling ring of death bore marks of the *Revenge's* rage. Four hundred Spaniards, by their own admission, had been killed, and quite six hundred wounded. One hundred Englishmen had thus accounted for a thousand Spaniards besides all those that sank!

Grenville now gave his last order: 'Sink me the

ship, Master-Gunner!' But the sailing master and flag-captain, both wounded, protesting that all lives should be saved to avenge the dead, manned the only remaining boat and made good terms with the Spanish admiral. Then Grenville was taken very carefully aboard Don Bazan's flagship, where he was received with every possible mark of admiration and respect. Don Bazan gave him his own cabin. The staff surgeon dressed his many wounds. The Spanish captains and military officers stood hat in hand, 'wondering at his courage and stout heart, for that he showed not any signs of faintness nor changing of his colour.' Grenville spoke Spanish very well and handsomely acknowledged the compliments they paid him. Then, gathering his ebbing strength for one last effort, he addressed them in words they have religiously recorded: ' "Here die I, Richard Grenville, with a joyful and quiet mind; for that I have ended my life as a true soldier ought to do, that hath fought for his country, queen, religion, and honour. Wherefore my soul most joyfully departeth out of this body." . . . And when he had said these and other suchlike words he gave up the ghost with a great and stout courage.'

Grenville's latest wish was that the *Revenge* and

he should die together; and, though he knew it not, he had this wish fulfilled. For, two weeks later, when Don Bazan had collected nearly a hundred more sail around him for the last stage home from the West Indies, a cyclone such as no living man remembered burst full on the crowded fleet. Not even the Great Armada lost more vessels than Don Bazan did in that wreck-engulfing week. No less than seventy went down. And with them sank the shattered *Revenge*, beside her own heroic dead.

Drake might be out of favor at court. The Queen might grumble at the sad extravagance of fleets. Diplomats might talk of untying Gordian knots that the sword was made to cut. Courtiers and politicians might wonder with which side to curry favor when it was an issue between two parties—peace or war. The great mass of ordinary landsmen might wonder why the 'sea-affair' was a thing they could not understand. But all this was only the mint and cummin of imperial things compared with the exalting deeds that Drake had done. For, once the English sea-dogs had shown the way to all America by breaking down the barriers of Spain, England had ceased to be merely an island in a northern sea and had become the mother country of such an empire and republic as neither record nor tradition can show the like of elsewhere.

And England felt the triumph. She thrilled with pregnant joy. Poet and proseman both gave voice to her delight. Hear this new note of exultation born of England's victory on the sea:

As God hath combined the sea and land into one globe, so their mutual assistance is necessary to secular happiness and glory. The sea covereth one-half of this patrimony of man. Thus should man at once lose the half of his inheritance if the art of navigation did not enable him to manage this untamed beast; and with the bridle of the winds and the saddle of his shipping make him serviceable. Now for the services of the sea, they are innumerable: it is the great purveyor of the world's commodities; the conveyor of the excess of rivers; uniter, by traffique, of all nations; it presents the eye with divers colors and motions, and is, as it were with rich brooches, adorned with many islands. It is an open field for merchandise in peace; a pitched field for the most dreadful fights in war; yields diversity of fish and fowl for diet, material for wealth; medicine for sickness; pearls and jewels for adornment; the wonders of the Lord in the deep for all instruction; multiplicity of nature for contemplation; to the thirsty Earth fertile moisture; to distant friends pleasant meeting; to weary persons delightful refreshing; to studious minds a map of knowledge, a school of prayer, meditation, devotion, and sobriety; refuge to the distressed, portage to the merchant, customs to the prince, passage to the traveller; springs, lakes, and rivers to the Earth. It hath tempests and calms to chastise sinners and exercise the faith of seamen; manifold affections to stupefy the subtlest philosopher, maintaineth (as in Our Island) a wall of defence and watery garrison to guard the state. It entertains the Sun with vapors, the Stars with a natural looking-glass, the sky with clouds, the air with temperateness, the soil with suppleness, the rivers with tides, the hills with moisture, the valleys with fertility. But why should I longer detain you? The Sea yields action to the body, meditation to the mind, and the World to the World, by this art of arts — Navigation.

Well might this pious Englishman, the Reverend Samuel Purchas, exclaim with David: *Thy ways are in the Sea, and Thy paths in the great waters, and Thy footsteps are not known.*

The poets sang of Drake and England, too. Could his 'Encompassment of All the Worlde' be more happily admired than in these four short lines:

> The Stars of Heaven would thee proclaim
> If men here silent were.
> The Sun himself could not forget
> His fellow traveller.

What wonder that after Nombre de Dios and the Pacific, the West Indies and the Spanish Main, Cadiz and the Armada, what wonder, after this, that Shakespeare, English to the core, rings out:—

This royal throne of kings, this sceptred isle,
This earth of majesty, this seat of Mars,
This other Eden, demi-paradise;
This fortress built by nature for herself
Against infection and the hand of war;
This happy breed of men, this little world;
This precious stone set in the silver sea,
Which serves it in the office of a wall,
Or as a moat defensive to a house,
Against the envy of less happy lands:
This blessed plot, this earth, this realm, this England.

. . . .

This England never did, nor never shall,
Lie at the proud foot of a conqueror,
But when it first did help to wound itself.
Now these her princes are come home again,
Come the three corners of the world in arms
And we shall shock them. Nought shall make us rue,
If England to herself do rest but true.

CHAPTER XI

RALEIGH AND THE VISION OF THE WEST

CONQUERORS first, prospectors second, then the pioneers: that is the order of those by whom America was opened up for English-speaking people. No Elizabethan colonies took root. Therefore the age of Elizabethan sea-dogs was one of conquerors and prospectors, not one of pioneering colonists at all.

Spain and Portugal alone founded sixteenth-century colonies that have had a continuous life from those days to our own. Virginia and New England, like New France, only began as permanent settlements after Drake and Queen Elizabeth were dead: Virginia in 1607, New France in 1608, New England in 1620.

It is true that Drake and his sea-dogs were prospectors in their way. So were the soldiers, gentlemen-adventurers, and fighting traders in theirs. On the other hand, some of the prospectors themselves belong to the class of conquerors, while many would have gladly been the pioneers of permanent colonies. Nevertheless the prospectors form a separate class; and Sir Walter Raleigh, though an adventurer in every other way as well, is undoubtedly their chief. His colonies failed. He never found his El Dorado. He died a ruined and neglected man. But still he was the chief of those whom we can only call prospectors, first, because they tried their fortune ashore, one step beyond the conquering sea-dogs, and, secondly, because their fortune failed them just one step short of where the pioneering colonists began.

> A man so various that he seemed to be
> Not one but all mankind's epitome

is a description written about a very different character. But it is really much more appropriate to Sir Walter Raleigh. Courtier and would-be colonizer, soldier and sailor, statesman and scholar, poet and master of prose, Raleigh had one ruling passion greater than all the rest combined. In a letter about America to Sir Robert Cecil, the son of Queen Elizabeth's principal minister of state, Lord Burleigh, he expressed this great determined purpose of his life: *I shall yet live to see it an In-glishe nation*. He had other interests in abundance, perhaps in superabundance; and he had much more than the usual temptations to live the life of fashion with just enough of public duty to satisfy both the queen and the very least that is implied by the motto *Noblesse oblige*. He was splendidly handsome and tall, a perfect blend of strength and grace, full of deep, romantic interest in great things far and near: the very man whom women dote on. And yet, through all the seductions of the Court and all the storm and stress of Europe, he steadily pursued the vision of that West which he would make 'an Inglishe nation.'

He left Oxford as an undergraduate to serve the Huguenots in France under Admiral Coligny and the Protestants in Holland under William of Orange. Like Hawkins and Drake, he hated Spain with all his heart and paid off many a score against her by killing Spanish troops at Smerwick during an Irish campaign marked by ruthless slaughter on both sides. On his return to England he soon attracted the charmed attention of the queen. His spreading his cloak for her to tread on, lest she might wet her feet, is one of those stories which ought to be true if it's not. In any case he won the royal favor, was granted monopolies, promotion, and estates, and launched upon the full flood-stream of fortune.

He was not yet thirty when he obtained for his half-brother, Sir Humphrey Gilbert, then a man of thirty-eight, a royal commission 'to inhabit and possess all remote and Heathen lands not in the possession of any Christian prince.' The draft of Gilbert's original prospectus, dated at London, the 6th of November, 1577, and still kept there in the Record Office, is an appeal to Elizabeth in which he proposed 'to discover and inhabit some strange place.' Gilbert was a soldier and knew what fighting meant; so he likewise proposed 'to set forth certain ships of war to the New Land, which, with your good licence, I will undertake without your Majesty's charge. . . . The New Land fish is a principal and rich and everywhere vendible merchandise; and by the gain thereof shipping, victual, munition, and the transporting of five or six thousand soldiers may be defrayed.'

But Gilbert's associates cared nothing for fish and everything for gold. He went to the West Indies, lost a ship, and returned without a fortune. Next year he was forbidden to repeat the experiment.

The project then languished until the fatal voyage of 1583, when Gilbert set sail with six vessels, intending to occupy Newfoundland as the base from which to colonize southwards until an armed New England should meet and beat New Spain. How vast his scheme! How pitiful its execution! And yet how immeasurably beyond his wildest dreams the actual development to-day! Gilbert was not a sea-dog but a soldier with an uncanny reputation for being a regular Jonah who 'had no good hap at sea.' He was also passionately self-willed, and Elizabeth had doubts about the propriety of backing him. But she sent him a gilt anchor by way of good luck and off he went in June, financed chiefly by Raleigh, whose name was given to the flagship.

Gilbert's adventure never got beyond its base in Newfoundland. His ship the *Delight* was wrecked. The crew of the *Raleigh* mutinied and ran her home to England. The other four vessels held on. But the men, for the most part, were neither good soldiers, good sailors, nor yet good colonists, but ne'er-do-wells and desperadoes. By September the expedition was returning broken down. Gilbert, furious at the sailors' hints that he was just a little sea-shy, would persist in sticking

14

to the Lilliputian ten-ton *Squirrel*, which was woefully top-hampered with guns and stores. Before leaving Newfoundland he was implored to abandon her and bring her crew aboard a bigger craft. But no. 'Do not fear,' he answered; 'we are as near to Heaven by sea as land.' One wild night off the Azores the *Squirrel* foundered with all hands.

Amadas and Barlow sailed in 1584. Prospecting for Sir Walter Raleigh, they discovered several harbors in North Carolina, then part of the vast 'plantation' of Virginia. Roanoke Island, Pamlico and Albemarle Sounds, as well as the intervening waters, were all explored with enthusiastic thoroughness and zeal. Barlow, a skipper who was handy with his pen, described the scent of that fragrant summer land in terms which attracted the attention of Bacon at the time and of Dryden a century later. The royal charter authorizing Raleigh to take what he could find in this strange land had a clause granting his prospective colonists 'all the privileges of free denizens and persons native of England in such ample manner as if they were born and personally resident in our said realm of England.'

Next year Sir Richard Grenville, who was

Raleigh's cousin, convoyed out to Roanoke the little colony which Ralph Lane governed and which, as we have seen in an earlier chapter, Drake took home discomfited in 1586. There might have been a story to tell of successful colonization, instead of failure, if Drake had kept away from Roanoke that year or if he had tarried a few days longer. For no sooner had the colony departed in Drake's vessels than a ship sent out by Sir Walter Raleigh, 'freighted with all maner of things in most plentiful maner,' arrived at Roanoke; and 'after some time spent in seeking our Colony up in the countrey, and not finding them, returned with all the aforesayd provision into England.' About a fortnight later Sir Richard Grenville himself arrived with three ships. Not wishing to lose possession of the country where he had planted a colony the year before, he 'landed fifteene men in the Isle of Roanoak, furnished plentifully with all maner of provision for two yeeres, and so departed for England.' Grenville unfortunately had burnt an Indian town and all its standing corn because the Indians had stolen a silver cup. Lane, too, had been severe in dealing with the natives and they had turned from friends to foes. These and other facts were carefully recorded on the spot by the official chronicler, Thomas Harriot, better known as a mathematician.

Among the captains who had come out under Grenville in 1585 was Thomas Cavendish, a young and daring gentleman-adventurer, greatly distinguished as such even in that adventurous age, and the second English leader to circumnavigate the globe. When Drake was taking Lane's men home in June, 1586, Cavendish was making the final preparations for a two-year voyage. He sailed mostly along the route marked out by Drake, and many of his adventures were of much the same kind. His prime object was to make the voyage pay a handsome dividend. But he did notable service in clipping the wings of Spain. He raided the shipping off Chile and Peru, took the Spanish flagship, the famous *Santa Anna*, off the coast of California, and on his return home in 1588 had the satisfaction of reporting: 'I burned and sank nineteen sail of ships, both small and great; and all the villages and towns that ever I landed at I burned and spoiled.'

While Cavendish was preying on Spanish treasure in America, and Drake was 'singeing the King of Spain's beard' in Europe, Raleigh still pursued his colonizing plans. In 1587 John White and twelve associates received incorporation as the 'Governor and Assistants of the City of Ralegh in Virginia.' The fortunes of this ambitious city were not unlike those of many another 'boomed' and 'busted' city of much more recent date. No time was lost in beginning. Three ships arrived at Roanoke on the 22nd of July, 1587. Every effort was made to find the fifteen men left behind the year before by Grenville to hold possession for the Queen. Mounds of earth, which may even now be traced, so piously have their last remains been cared for, marked the site of the fort. From natives of Croatoan Island the newcomers learned that Grenville's men had been murdered by hostile Indians.

One native friend was found in Manteo, a chief whom Barlow had taken to England and Grenville had brought back. Manteo was now living with his own tribe of sea-coast Indians on Croatoan Island. But the mischief between red and white had been begun; and though Manteo had been baptized and was recognized as 'The Lord of Roanoke' the races were becoming fatally estranged.

After a month Governor White went home for more men and supplies, leaving most of the colonists at Roanoke. He found Elizabeth, Raleigh, and the rest all working to meet the Great Armada. Yet, even during the following year, the momentous year of 1588, Raleigh managed to spare two pinnaces, with fifteen colonists aboard, well provided with all that was most needed. A Spanish squadron, however, forced both pinnaces to run back for their lives. After this frustrated attempt two more years passed before White could again sail for Virginia. In August, 1590, his trumpeter sounded all the old familiar English calls as he approached the little fort. No answer came. The colony was lost for ever. White had arranged that if the colonists should be obliged to move away they should carve the name of the new settlement on the fort or surrounding trees, and that if there was either danger or distress they should cut a cross above. The one word CROATOAN was all White ever found. There was no cross. White's beloved colony, White's favorite daughter and her little girl, were perhaps in hiding. But supplies were running short. White was a mere passenger on board the ship that brought him; and the crew were getting impatient, so impatient for 'refreshment' and a Spanish prize that they sailed past Croatoan, refusing to stop a single hour.

Perhaps White learnt more than is recorded and was satisfied that all the colonists were dead. Perhaps not. Nobody knows. Only a wandering tradition comes out of that impenetrable mystery and circles round the not impossible romance of young Virginia Dare. Her father was one of White's twelve 'Assistants.' Her mother, Eleanor, was White's daughter. Virginia herself, the first of all true 'native-born' Americans, was born on the 18th of August, 1587. Perhaps Manteo, 'Lord of Roanoke,' saved the whole family whose name has been commemorated by that of the North Carolina county of Dare. Perhaps Virginia Dare alone survived to be an 'Indian Queen' about the time the first permanent Anglo-American colony was founded in 1607, twenty years after her birth. Who knows?

These twenty sundering years, from the end of this abortive colony in 1587 to the beginning of the first permanent colony in 1607, constitute a period that saw the close of one age and the opening of another in every relation of Anglo-American affairs.

Nor was it only in Anglo-American affairs that change was rife. 'The Honourable East India

Company' entered upon its wonderful career. Shakespeare began to write his immortal plays. The chosen translators began their work on the Authorized Version of the English Bible. The Puritans were becoming a force within the body politic as well as in religion. Ulster was 'planted' with Englishmen and Lowland Scots. In the midst of all these changes the great Queen, grown old and very lonely, died in 1603; and with her ended the glorious Tudor dynasty of England. James, pusillanimous and pedantic son of Darnley and Mary Queen of Scots, ascended the throne as the first of the sinister Stuarts, and, truckling to vindictive Spain, threw Raleigh into prison under suspended sentence of death.

There was a break of no less than fifteen years in English efforts to colonize America. Nothing was tried between the last attempt at Roanoke in 1587 and the first attempt in Massachusetts in 1602, when thirty-two people sailed from England with Bartholomew Gosnold, formerly a skipper in Raleigh's employ. Gosnold made straight for the coast of Maine, which he sighted in May. He then coasted south to Cape Cod. Continuing south he entered Buzzard's Bay, where he landed on Cutty-hunk Island. Here, on a little island in a lake —

an island within an island — he built a fort round
which the colony was expected to grow.   But supplies began to run out.   There was bad blood over
the proper division of what remained.   The would-
be colonists could not agree with those who had no
intention of staying behind.   The result was that
the entire project had to be given up.   Gosnold
sailed home with the whole disgusted crew and a
cargo of sassafras and cedar.   Such was the first
prospecting ever done for what is now New England.

The following year, 1603, just after the death of
Queen Elizabeth, some merchant-venturers of
Bristol sent out two vessels under Martin Pring.
Like Gosnold, Pring first made the coast of Maine
and then felt his way south.   Unlike Gosnold,
however, he 'bore into the great Gulfe' of Massachusetts Bay, where he took in a cargo of sassafras
at Plymouth Harbor.   But that was all the prospecting done this time.   There was no attempt at
colonizing.

Two years later another prospector was sent out
by a more important company.   The Earl of
Southampton and Sir Ferdinando Gorges were the
chief promoters of this enterprise.   Gorges, as
'Lord Proprietary of the Province of Maine,' is a

well-known character in the subsequent history of New England. Lord Southampton, as Shakespeare's only patron and greatest personal friend, is forever famous through the world. The chief prospector chosen by the company was George Weymouth, who landed on the coast of Maine, explored a little of the surrounding country, kidnapped five Indians, and returned to England with a glowing account of what he had seen.

The cumulative effect of the three expeditions of Gosnold, Pring, and Weymouth was a revival of interest in colonization. Prominent men soon got together and formed two companies which were formally chartered by King James on the 10th of April, 1606. The 'first' or 'southern colony,' which came to be known as the London Company because most of its members lived there, was authorized to make its 'first plantation at any place upon the coast of Virginia or America between the four-and-thirty and one-and-forty degrees of latitude.' The northern or 'second colony,' afterwards called the Plymouth Company, was authorized to settle any place between 38° and 45° north, thus overlapping both the first company to the south and the French to the north.

In the summer of the same year, 1606, Henry

Challons took two ships of the Plymouth Company round by the West Indies, where he was caught in a fog by the Spaniards.   Later in the season Pring went out and explored 'North Virginia.'   In May, 1607, a hundred and twenty men, under George Popham, started to colonize this 'North Virginia.' In August they landed in Maine at the mouth of the Kennebec, where they built a fort, some houses, and a pinnace.   Finding themselves short of provisions, two-thirds of their number returned to England late in the same year.   The remaining third passed a terrible winter.   Popham died, and Raleigh Gilbert succeeded him as governor. When spring came all the survivors of the colony sailed home in the pinnace they had built and the enterprise was abandoned.   The reports of the colonists, after their winter in Maine, were to the effect that the second or northern colony was 'not habitable for Englishmen.'

In the meantime the permanent foundation of the first or southern colony, the real Virginia, was well under way.   The same number of intending emigrants went out, a hundred and twenty.   On the 26th of April, 1607, 'about four a-clocke in the morning, wee descried the Land of Virginia: the same day wee entered into the Bay of Chesupioc'

[Chesapeake]. Thus begins the tale of Captain John Smith, of the founding of Jamestown, and of a permanent Virginia, the first of the future United States.

Now that we have seen one spot in vast America really become the promise of the 'Inglishe nation' which Raleigh had longed for, we must return once more to Raleigh himself as, mocked by his tantalizing vision, he looked out on a changing world from his secular Mount Pisgah in the prison Tower of London.

By this time he had felt both extremes of fortune to the full. During the travesty of justice at his trial the attorney-general, having no sound argument, covered him with slanderous abuse. These are three of the false accusations on which he was condemned to death: 'Viperous traitor,' 'damnable atheist,' and 'spider of hell.' Hawkins, Drake, Frobisher, and Grenville, all were dead. So Raleigh, last of the great Elizabethan lions, was caged and baited for the sport of Spain.

Six of his twelve years of imprisonment were lightened by the companionship of his wife, Elizabeth Throgmorton, most beautiful of all the late

SIR WALTER RALEIGH, ABOUT THIRTY-FOUR YEARS OF AGE

Painting attributed to Federigo Zucchero. In the National Portrait Gallery, London, England.

Queen's maids of honor. Another solace was the
History of the World, the writing of which set his
mind free to wander forth at will although his body
stayed behind the bars. But the contrast was too
poignant not to wring this cry of anguish from his
preface: 'Yet when we once come in sight of the
Port of death, to which all winds drive us, and
when by letting fall that fatal Anchor, which can
never be weighed again, the navigation of this life
takes end: Then it is, I say, that our own cogitations (those sad and severe cogitations, formerly
beaten from us by our health and felicity) return
again, and pay us to the uttermost for all the
pleasing passages of our life past.'

At length, in the spring of 1616, Raleigh was
released, though still unpardoned. He and his
devoted wife immediately put all that remained
of their fortune into a new venture. Twenty years
before this he thought he could make 'Discovery of
the mighty, rich, and beautiful Empire of Guiana,
and of that great and golden city, which the Spaniards call El Dorado, and the natives call Manoa.'
Now he would go back to find the El Dorado of
his dreams, somewhere inland, that mysterious
Manoa among those southern Mountains of Bright
Stones which lay behind the Spanish Main.   The

king's cupidity was roused; and so, in 1617, Raleigh was commissioned as the admiral of fourteen sail. In November he arrived off the coast that guarded all the fabled wealth still lying undiscovered in the far recesses of the Orinocan wilds. *Guiana, Manoa, El Dorado* — the inland voices called him on.

But Spaniards barred the way; and Raleigh, defying the instructions of the King, attacked them. The English force was far too weak and disaster followed. Raleigh's son and heir was killed and his lieutenant committed suicide. His men began to mutiny. Spanish troops and ships came closing in; and the forlorn remnant of the expedition on which such hopes were built went straggling home to England. There Raleigh was arrested and sent to the block on the 29th of October, 1618. He had played the great game of life-and-death and lost it. When he mounted the scaffold, he asked to see the axe. Feeling the edge, he smiled and said: ''Tis a sharp medicine, but a cure for all diseases.' Then he bared his neck and died like one who had served the Great Queen as her Captain of the Guard.

CHAPTER XII

DRAKE'S END

DRAKE in disfavor after 1589 seems a contradiction that nothing can explain. It can, however, be quite easily explained, though never explained away. He had simply failed to make the Lisbon Expedition pay — a heinous offence in days when the navy was as much a revenue department as the customs or excise. He had also failed to take Lisbon itself. The reasons why mattered nothing either to the disappointed government or to the general public.

But, six years later, in 1595, when Drake was fifty and Hawkins sixty-three, England called on them both to strike another blow at Spain. Elizabeth was helping Henry IV of France against the League of French and Spanish Catholics. Henry, astute as he was gallant, had found Paris 'worth a mass' and, to Elizabeth's dismay, had gone straight over to the Church of Rome with terms of toleration for the Huguenots. The war against the Holy League, however, had not yet ended. The effect of Henry's conversion was to make a more united France against the encroaching power of Spain. And every eye in England was soon turned on Drake and Hawkins for a stroke at Spanish power beyond the sea.

Drake and Hawkins formed a most unhappy combination, made worse by the fact that Hawkins, now old beyond his years, soured by misfortune, and staled for the sea by long spells of office work, was put in as a check on Drake, in whom Elizabeth had lost her former confidence. Sir Thomas Baskerville was to command the troops. Here, at least, no better choice could have possibly been made. Baskerville had fought with rare distinction in the Brest campaign and before that in the Netherlands.

There was the usual hesitation about letting the fleet go far from home. The 'purely defensive' school was still strong; Elizabeth in certain moods belonged to it; and an incident which took place about this time seemed to give weight to the arguments of the defensivists. A small Spanish force, obliged to find water and provisions in a hurry, put into Mousehole in Cornwall and, finding no op-

position, burnt several villages down to the ground.
The moment these Spaniards heard that Drake
and Hawkins were at Plymouth they decamped.
But this ridiculous raid threw the country into
doubt or consternation. Elizabeth was as brave
as a lion for herself. But she never grasped the
meaning of naval strategy, and she was supersen-
sitive to any strong general opinion, however false.
Drake and Hawkins, with Baskerville's troops (all
in transports) and many supply vessels for the
West India voyage, were ordered to cruise about
Ireland and Spain looking for enemies. The
admirals at once pointed out that this was the work
of the Channel Fleet, not that of a joint expedition
bound for America. Then, just as the Queen was
penning an angry reply, she received a letter from
Drake, saying that the chief Spanish treasure ship
from Mexico had been seen in Porto Rico little
better than a wreck, and that there was time to
take her if they could only sail at once. The expedition was on the usual joint-stock lines and
Elizabeth was the principal shareholder. She
swallowed the bait whole; and sent sailing orders
down to Plymouth by return.

And so, on the 28th of August, 1595, twenty-five
hundred men in twenty-seven vessels sailed out,

15

bound for New Spain. Surprise was essential; for New Spain, taught by repeated experience, was well armed; and twenty-five hundred men were less formidable now than five hundred twenty years before. Arrived at the Canaries, Las Palmas was found too strong to carry by immediate assault; and Drake had no time to attack it in form. He was two months late already; so he determined to push on to the West Indies.

When Drake reached Porto Rico, he found the Spanish in a measure forewarned and forearmed. Though he astonished the garrison by standing boldly into the harbor and dropping anchor close to a masked battery, the real surprise was now against him. The Spanish gunners got the range to an inch, brought down the flagship's mizzen, knocked Drake's chair from under him, killed two senior officers beside him, and wounded many more. In the meantime Hawkins, worn out by his exertions, had died. This reception, added to the previous failures and the astonishing strength of Porto Rico, produced a most depressing effect. Drake weighed anchor and went out. He was soon back in a new place, cleverly shielded from the Spanish guns by a couple of islands. After some more manœuvres he attacked the Spanish fleet with fire-

balls and by boarding. When a burning frigate
lit up the whole wild scene, the Spanish gunners
and musketeers poured into the English ships such
a concentrated fire that Drake was compelled
to retreat. He next tried the daring plan of running straight into the harbor, where there might
still be a chance. But the Spaniards sank four of
their own valuable vessels in the harbor mouth —
guns, stores, and all — just in the nick of time, and
thus completely barred the way.

Foiled again, Drake dashed for the mainland,
seized La Hacha, burnt it, ravaged the surrounding country, and got away with a successful
haul of treasure; then he seized Santa Marta
and Nombre de Dios, both of which were found
nearly empty. The whole of New Spain was taking the alarm — *The Dragon's back again!* Meanwhile a fleet of more than twice Drake's strength
was coming out from Spain to attack him in the
rear. Nor was this all, for Baskerville and his
soldiers, who had landed at Nombre de Dios and
started overland, were in full retreat along the
road from Panama, having found an impregnable
Spanish position on the way. It was a sad beginning for 1596, the centennial year of England's
first connection with America.

'Since our return from Panama he never carried mirth nor joy in his face,' wrote one of Baskerville's officers who was constantly near Drake. A council of war was called and Drake, making the best of it, asked which they would have, Truxillo, the port of Honduras, or the 'golden towns' round about Lake Nicaragua. 'Both,' answered Baskerville, 'one after the other.' So the course was laid for San Juan on the Nicaragua coast. A head wind forced Drake to anchor under the island of Veragua, a hundred and twenty-five miles west of Nombre de Dios Bay and right in the deadliest part of that fever-stricken coast. The men began to sicken and die off. Drake complained at table that the place had changed for the worse. His earlier memories of New Spain were of a land like a 'pleasant and delicious arbour' very different from the 'vast and desert wilderness' he felt all round him now. The wind held foul. More and more men lay dead or dying. At last Drake himself, the man of iron constitution and steel nerves, fell ill and had to keep his cabin. Then reports were handed in to say the stores were running low and that there would soon be too few hands to man the ships. On this he gave the order to weigh and 'take the wind as God had sent it.'

So they stood out from that pestilential Mosquito Gulf and came to anchor in the fine harbor of Puerto Bello, which the Spaniards had chosen to replace the one at Nombre de Dios, twenty miles east. Here, in the night of the 27th of January, Drake suddenly sprang out of his berth, dressed himself, and raved of battles, fleets, Armadas, Plymouth Hoe, and plots against his own command. The frenzy passed away. He fell exhausted, and was lifted back to bed again. Then 'like a Christian, he yielded up his spirit quietly.'

His funeral rites befitted his renown. The great new Spanish fort of Puerto Bello was given to the flames, as were nearly all the Spanish prizes, and even two of his own English ships; for there were now no sailors left to man them. Thus, amid the thunder of the guns whose voice he knew so well, and surrounded by consuming pyres afloat and on the shore, his body was committed to the deep, while muffled drums rolled out their last salute and trumpets wailed his requiem.

APPENDIX

NOTE ON TUDOR SHIPPING

In the sixteenth century there was no hard-and-fast distinction between naval and all other craft. The sovereign had his own fighting vessels; and in the course of the seventeenth century these gradually evolved into a Royal Navy maintained entirely by the country as a whole and devoted solely to the national defence. But in earlier days this modern system was difficult everywhere and impossible in England. The English monarch, for all his power, had no means of keeping up a great army and navy without the help of Parliament and the general consent of the people. The Crown had great estates and revenues; but nothing like enough to make war on a national scale. Consequently king and people went into partnership, sometimes in peace as well as war. When fighting stopped, and no danger seemed to threaten, the king would use his men-of-war in trade himself, or even hire them out to merchants. The merchants, for their part, furnished vessels to the king in time of war. Except as supply ships, however, these auxiliaries were never a great success. The privateers built expressly for fighting were the only ships that could approach the men-of-war.

Yet, strangely enough, King Henry's first modern men-of-war grew out of a merchant-ship model, and a foreign one at that. Throughout ancient and mediæval times the 'long ship' was the man-of-war while the 'round ship' was the merchantman. But the long ship was always some sort of galley, which, as we have seen repeatedly, depended on its oars and used sails only occasionally, and then not in action, while the round ship was built to carry cargo and to go under sail. The Italian naval architects, then the most scientific in the world, were trying to evolve two types of vessel: one that could act as light cavalry on the wings of a galley fleet, the other that could carry big cargoes safely through the pirate-haunted seas. In both types sail power and fighting power were essential. Finally a compromise resulted and the galleasse appeared. The galleasse was a hybrid between the galley and the sailing vessel, between the 'long ship' that was several times as long as it was broad and the 'round ship' that was only two or three times as long as its beam. Then, as the oceanic routes gained on those of the inland seas, and as oceanic sea power gained in the same proportion, the galleon appeared. The galleon had no oars at all, as the hybrid galleasses had, and it gained more in sail power than it lost by dropping oars. It was, in fact, the direct progenitor of the old three-decker which some people still alive can well remember.

At the time the Cabots and Columbus were discovering America the Venetians had evolved the merchant-galleasse for their trade with London: they called it, indeed, the *galleazza di Londra*. Then, by the time Henry VIII was building his new modern navy, the real galleon had been evolved (out of the Italian new war- and older merchant-galleasses) by England, France, and Scotland; but by England best of all. In original ideas of naval architecture England was generally behind, as she continued to be till well within living memory. Nelson's captains competed eagerly for the command of French prizes, which were better built and from superior designs. The American frigates of 1812 were incomparably better than the corresponding classes in the British service were; and so on in many other instances. But, in spite of being rather slow, conservative, and rule-of-thumb, the English were already beginning to develop a national sea-sense far beyond that of any other people. They could not, indeed, do otherwise and live. Henry's policy, England's position, the dawn of oceanic strategy, and the discovery of America, all combined to make her navy by far the most important single factor in England's problems with the world at large. As with the British Empire now, so with England then: the choice lay between her being either first or nowhere.

Henry's reasoning and his people's instinct having led to the same resolve, everyone with any sea-sense, especially shipwrights like Fletcher of Rye, began working towards the best types then obtainable. There were mistakes in plenty. The theory of naval architecture in England was never both sound and strong enough to get its own way against all opposition. But with the issue of life and death always dependent on sea power, and with so many men of every class following the sea, there was at all events the biggest rough-and-tumble school of practical seamanship that any leading country ever had. The two essential steps were quickly taken: first, from oared galleys with very little sail power to the hybrid galleasse with much more sail and much less in the way of oars; secondly, from this to the purely sailing galleon.

With the galleon we enter the age of sailing tactics which decided the fate of the oversea world. This momentous age began with Drake and the English galleon. It ended with Nelson and the first-rate, three-decker, ship-of-the-line. But it was one throughout; for its beginning differed from its end no more than a father differs from his son.

One famous Tudor vessel deserves some special notice, not because of her excellence but because of her defects. The *Henry Grace à Dieu,* or *Great Harry* as she was generally called, launched in 1514, was Henry's own flagship on his way to the Field of the Cloth of Gold in 1520. She had a gala suit of sails and pennants, all made of damasked cloth of gold. Her quarters, sides, and tops were emblazoned with heraldic targets. Court artists painted her to show His Majesty on board wearing cloth of gold, edged with the royal ermine; as well as bright crimson jacket, sleeves, and breeches, with a long white feather in his cap. Doubtless, too, His Majesty of France paid her all the proper compliments; while every man who was then what reporters are to-day talked her up to the top of his bent. No single vessel ever had greater publicity till the famous first *Dreadnought* of our own day appeared in the British navy nearly four hundred years later.

But the much advertised *Great Harry* was not a mighty prototype of a world-wide-copied class of battleships like the modern *Dreadnought*. With her lavish decorations, her towering superstructures fore and aft, and her general aping of a floating castle, she was the wonder of all the landsmen in her own age, as she has been the delight of picturesque historians ever since. But she marked no advance in naval architecture, rather the reverse. She was the last great English ship of mediæval times. Twenty-five years after the Field of the Cloth of Gold, Henry was commanding another English fleet, the first of modern times, and therefore one in which the out-of-date *Great Harry* had no proper place at all. She was absurdly top-hampered and over-gunned. And, for all her thousand tons, she must have bucketed about in the chops of the Channel with the same sort of hobby-horse, see-sawing pitch that bothered Captain Concas in 1893 when sailing an exact reproduction of Columbus's flagship, the *Santa Maria*, across the North Atlantic to the great World's Fair at Chicago.

In her own day the galleon was the 'great ship,' 'capital ship,' 'ship-of-the-line-of-battle,' or 'battleship' on which the main fight turned. But just as our modern fleets require three principal kinds of vessels — battleships, cruisers, and 'mosquito' craft — so did the fleets of Henry and Elizabeth. The galleon did the same work as the old three-decker of Nelson's time or the battleship of to-day. The 'pinnace' (quite different from more modern pinnaces) was the frigate or the cruiser. And, in Henry VIII's fleet of 1545, the 'row-barge' was the principal 'mosquito' craft, like the modern torpedo-boat, destroyer, or even submarine. Of course the correspondence is far from being complete in any class.

The English galleon gradually developed more sail and gun power as well as handiness in action. Broadside fire began. When used against the Armada, it had grown very powerful indeed. At that time the best guns, some of which are still in existence, were nearly as good as those at Trafalgar or aboard the smart American frigates that did so well in '1812.' When galleon broadsides were fired from more than a single deck, the lower ones took enemy craft between wind and water very nicely. In the English navy the portholes had been cut so as to let the guns be pointed with considerable freedom, up or down, right or left. The huge top-hampering 'castles' and other soldier-engineering works on deck were modified or got rid of, while more canvas was used and to much better purpose.

The pinnace showed the same sort of improvement during the same period — from Drake's birth under Henry VIII in 1545 to the zenith of his career as a sea-dog in 1588. This progenitor of the frigate and the cruiser was itself descended from the long-boat of the Norsemen and still used oars as occasion served. But the sea-dogs made it primarily a sailing vessel of anything up to a hundred tons and generally averaging over fifty. A smart pinnace, with its long, low, clean-run hull, if well handled under its Elizabethan fighting canvas of foresail and main topsail, could play round

a Spanish galleasse or absurdly castled galleon like a
lancer on a well-trained charger round a musketeer
astraddle on a cart horse.[1] Henry's pinnaces still had
lateen sails copied from Italian models. Elizabeth's
had square sails prophetic of the frigate's. Henry's
had one or a very few small guns. Elizabeth's had as
many as sixteen, some of medium size, in a hundred-
tonner.

The 'mosquito' fleet of Henry's time was represented
by 'row-barges' of his own invention. Now that the
pinnace was growing in size and sail power, while
shedding half its oars, some new small rowing craft
was wanted, during that period of groping transition,
to act as a tender or to do 'mosquito' work in action.
The mere fact that Henry VIII placed no dependence
on oars except for this smallest type shows how far
he had got on the road towards the broadside-sailing-
ship fleet. On the 16th of July, 1541, the Spanish Naval
Attaché (as we should call him now) reported to Charles
V that Henry had begun 'to have new oared vessels
built after his own design.' Four years later these
same 'row-barges' — long, light, and very handy —
hung round the sterns of the retreating Italian galleys
in the French fleet to very good purpose, plying them
with bow-chasers and the two broadside guns, till

[1] Fuller in his *Worthies* (1662) writes:
'Many were the wit-combats betwixt him [Shakespeare] and
Ben Jonson, which two I beheld like a Spanish great galleon and an
English man-of-war: Master Jonson (like the former) was built far
higher in learning, solid but slow in his performances. Shakespeare,
like the English man-of-war, lesser in bulk, but lighter in sailing,
could turn with all tides, tack about, and take advantage of all
winds by the quickness of his wit and invention.'

Strozzi, the Italian galley-admiral, turned back on them in fury, only to see them slip away in perfect order and with complete immunity.

By the time of the Armada the mosquito fleet had outgrown these little rowing craft and had become more oceanic. But names, types, and the evolution of one type from another, with the application of the same name to changed and changing types, all tend to confusion unless the subject is followed in such detail as is impossible here.

The fleets of Henry VIII and of Elizabeth did far more to improve both the theory and practice of naval gunnery than all the fleets in the world did from the death of Drake to the adoption of rifled ordnance within the memory of living men. Henry's textbook of artillery, republished in 1588, the year of the Armada, contains very practical diagrams for finding the range at sea by means of the gunner's half circle — yet we now think range-finding a very modern thing indeed. There are also full directions for making common and even something like shrapnel shells, 'star shells' to light up the enemy at night, armor-piercing arrows shot out of muskets, 'wild-fire' grenades, and many other ultra-modern devices.

Henry established Woolwich Dockyard, second to none both then and now, as well as Trinity House, which presently began to undertake the duties it still discharges by supervising all aids to navigation round the British Isles. The use of quadrants, telescopes, and maps on Mercator's projection all began in the reign of Elizabeth, as did many other inventions, adaptations, handy wrinkles, and vital changes in strategy and tactics. Taken together, these improvements may well make us of the twentieth century wonder whether we are so very much superior to the comrades of Henry, Elizabeth, Shakespeare, Bacon, Raleigh, and Drake.

BIBLIOGRAPHICAL NOTE

A COMPLETE bibliography concerned with the first
century of Anglo-American affairs (1496–1596) would
more than fill the present volume. But really infor-
matory books about the sea-dogs proper are very
few indeed, while good books of any kind are none too
common.

Taking this first century as a whole, the general
reader cannot do better than look up the third volume
of Justin Winsor's *Narrative and Critical History of
America* (1884) and the first volume of Avery's *History
of the United States and its People* (1904). Both give
elaborate references to documents and books, but
neither professes to be at all expert in naval or nautical
matters, and a good deal has been written since.

THE CABOTS. Cabot literature is full of conjecture
and controversy. G. P. Winship's *Cabot Bibliography*
(1900) is a good guide to all but recent works. Nicholls'
Remarkable Life of Sebastian Cabot (1869) shows more
zeal than discretion. Harrisse's *John Cabot and his son
Sebastian* (1896) arranges the documents in scholarly
order but draws conclusions betraying a wonderful
ignorance of the coast. On the whole, Dr. S. E.
Dawson's very careful monographs in the *Transactions
of the Royal Society of Canada* (1894, 1896, 1897) are
the happiest blend of scholarship and local knowledge.

Neither the Cabots nor their crews appear to have written a word about their adventures and discoveries. Consequently the shifting threads of hearsay evidence soon became inextricably tangled. Biggar's *Precursors of Cartier* is an able and accurate work.

ELIZABETH. Turning to the patriot queen who had to steer England through so many storms and tortuous channels, we could find no better short guide to her political career than Beesley's volume about her in 'Twelve English Statesmen.' But the best all-round biography is *Queen Elizabeth* by Mandell Creighton, who also wrote an excellent epitome, called *The Age of Elizabeth*, for the 'Epochs of Modern History.' *Shakespeare's England*, published in 1916 by the Oxford University Press, is quite encyclopædic in its range.

LIFE AFLOAT. The general evolution of wooden sailing craft may be traced out in Part I of Sir George Holmes's convenient little treatise on *Ancient and Modern Ships*. There is no nautical dictionary devoted to Elizabethan times. But a good deal can be picked up from the two handy modern glossaries of Dana and Admiral Smyth, the first being an American author, the second a British one. Smyth's *Sailor's Word Book* has no alternative title. But Dana's *Seaman's Friend* is known in England under the name of *The Seaman's Manual*. Technicalities change so much more slowly afloat than ashore that even the ultra-modern editions of Paasch's magnificent polyglot dictionary, *From Keel to Truck*, still contain many nautical terms which will help the reader out of some of his difficulties.

The life of the sea-dogs, gentlemen-adventurers, and merchant-adventurers should be studied in Hakluyt's collection of *Principal Navigations, Voiages, Traffiques, and Discoveries;* though many of his original authors were landsmen while a few were civilians as well. This Elizabethan Odyssey, the great prose epic of the English race, was first published in a single solemn folio the year after the Armada — 1589. In the nineteenth century the Hakluyt Society reprinted and edited these *Navigations* and many similar works, though not without employing some editors who had no knowledge of the Navy or the sea. In 1893 E. J. Payne brought out a much handier edition of the *Voyages of the Elizabethan Seamen to America* which gives the very parts of Hakluyt we want for our present purpose, and gives them with a running accompaniment of pithy introductions and apposite footnotes. Nearly all historians are both landsmen and civilians whose sins of omission and commission are generally at their worst in naval and nautical affairs. But James Anthony Froude, whatever his other faults may be, did know something of life afloat, and his *English Seamen in the Sixteenth Century*, despite its ultra-Protestant tone, is well worth reading.

HAWKINS. *The Hawkins Voyages*, published by the Hakluyt Society, give the best collection of original accounts. They deal with three generations of this famous family and are prefaced by a good introduction. *A Sea-Dog of Devon*, by R. A. J. Walling (1907) is the best recent biography of Sir John Hawkins.

DRAKE. Politics, policy, trade, and colonization were all dependent on sea power; and just as the English Navy was by far the most important factor in solving the momentous New-World problems of that awakening age, so Drake was by far the most important factor in the English Navy. *The Worlde Encompassed by Sir Francis Drake* and *Sir Francis Drake his Voyage, 1595*, are two of the volumes edited by the Hakluyt Society. But these contemporary accounts of his famous fights and voyages do not bring out the supreme significance of his influence as an admiral, more especially in connection with the Spanish Armada. It must always be a matter of keen, though unavailing, regret that Admiral Mahan, the great American expositor of sea power, began with the seventeenth, not the sixteenth, century. But what Mahan left undone was afterwards done to admiration by Julian Corbett, Lecturer in History to the (British) Naval War College, whose *Drake and the Tudor Navy* (1912) is absolutely indispensable to any one who wishes to understand how England won her footing in America despite all that Spain could do to stop her. Corbett's *Drake* (1890) in the 'English Men of Action' series is an excellent epitome. But the larger book is very much the better. Many illuminative documents on *The Defeat of the Spanish Armada* were edited in 1894 by Corbett's predecessor, Sir John Laughton. The only other work that need be consulted is the first volume of *The Royal Navy: a History*, edited by Sir William Laird Clowes (1897). This is not so good an authority as Corbett; but it contains many details which help to round the story out, besides a wealth of illustration.

RALEIGH. Gilbert, Cavendish, Raleigh, and the other gentlemen-adventurers, were soldiers, not sailors; and if they had gone afloat two centuries later they would have fought at the head of marines, not of blue-

jackets; so their lives belong to a different kind of
biography from that concerned with Hawkins, Frobisher,
and Drake. Edwards's *Life of Sir Walter Raleigh* (1868)
contains all the most interesting letters and is a com-
petent work of its own kind. Oldys' edition of Raleigh's
Works still holds the field though its eight volumes were
published so long ago as 1829. Raleigh's *Discovery of
Guiana* is the favorite for reprinting. The Hakluyt
Society has produced an elaborate edition (1847) while
a very cheap and handy one has been published in
Cassell's National Library. W. G. Gosling's *Life of
Sir Humphry Gilbert* (1911) is the best recent work of
its kind.

The likeliest of all the Hakluyt Society's volumes, so
far as its title is concerned, is one which has hardly any
direct bearing on the subject of our book. Yet the
reader who is disappointed by the text of *Divers
Voyages to America* because it is not devoted to Elizabethan sea-dogs will be richly rewarded by the notes
on pages 116–141. These quaint bits of information
and advice were intended for quite another purpose.
But their transcriber's faith in their wider applicability
is fully justified. Here is the exact original heading
under which they first appeared: *Notes in Writing
besides More Privie by Mouth that were given by a Gentleman, Anno 1580, to M. Arthure Pette and to M. Charles
Jackman, sent by the Marchants of the Muscovie Com-
panie for the discouerie of the northeast strayte, not all-
together vnfit for some other enterprises of discouerie,
hereafter to bee taken in hande.*

See also in *The Encyclopædia Britannica*, 11th Ed.,
the articles on *Henry VIII, Elizabeth, Drake, Raleigh*, etc.

INDEX